SAINT
FRANCIS SOLANO

BOOKS BY MARY FABYAN WINDEATT

A Series of Twenty Books

Stories of the Saints for Young People ages 10 to 100

SAINT FRANCIS SOLANO

WONDER-WORKER OF THE NEW WORLD AND APOSTLE OF ARGENTINA AND PERU

By
Mary Fabyan Windeatt

Illustrated by
Gedge Harmon

TAN BOOKS AND PUBLISHERS, INC.
Rockford, Illinois 61105

Nihil Obstat: Francis J. Reine, S.T.D.
                   Censor Librorum

Imprimatur: ✠ Joseph E. Ritter, D.D.
                   Archbishop of Indianapolis
                   Feast of St. Francis Solano
                   July 13, 1946

The type in this book is the property of TAN Books and Publishers, Inc., and may not be reproduced, in whole or in part, without written permission from the Publisher. (This restriction applies only to reproduction of *this type*, not to quotations from the book.)

ISBN: 0-89555-431-3

Library of Congress Catalog Card No.: 93-61380

Printed and bound in the United States of America.

TAN BOOKS AND PUBLISHERS, INC.
P. O. Box 424
Rockford, Illinois 61105

1994

For
Jane Vollmuth.

CONTENTS

ACKNOWLEDGMENT

The author is deeply grateful to the Reverend Marion A. Habig, O.F.M., Secretary of the Franciscan General Delegation in New York City, for the use of books, pamphlets and original manuscripts concerning the life and times of Saint Francis Solano, Patron Saint of the Franciscan Missionary Union. Without his helpful comments and suggestions, this little book could not have been written.

SOUTH AMERICA AND CENTRAL AMERICA.

SAINT
FRANCIS SOLANO

CHAPTER 1

THE MAYOR'S SON

SCHOOL WAS over in the little Spanish town of Montilla on a sunny day in the year 1566. As the doors of the Jesuit college opened, a crowd of eager students poured down the steps and into the spacious grounds.

"Anybody want to go fishing?" cried one boy, tossing a battered textbook into the air and catching it with one hand.

A companion stared in mock dismay. "*Fishing?* After sitting down all day? Don't be silly, Peter. Let's have a ball game."

At once the would-be angler began to argue his case. Fishing was a restful pastime after six hours in a classroom. There was a little boat he knew, moored in a secret place down the river. It could hold five boys, maybe six. As for tackle and bait...

"No, no!" cried the others. "We want action!" And as someone threw a ball high over a tree, there was a mad scramble to catch it. Shouting and laughing rang from all sides, and soon even Peter had forgotten his previous interest in fishing.

1

"Ball game!" he called, as a fellow student came slowly down the front steps of the college. "Hurry up, Francis Solano. We're going over to the far field."

A smile lit up the newcomer's face, but he shook his head. "Thank you, Peter, not today. I have to look after some very important business."

Peter shrugged his shoulders and trotted off to join his companions, who had almost reached the main gate. Soon the carefree group had disappeared, and comparative quiet descended upon the deserted school grounds.

For a moment the newcomer stood looking after his friends, his dark eyes thoughtful. He had told the truth about his important business. Today, this very afternoon, he was going to tell his parents of the decision he had reached after weeks of prayerful thought: that God was calling him to be a priest.

"A *Franciscan* priest," he told himself happily, "and here in the friary in Montilla."

As he made his way toward the gate, the boy's mind was busy with the wonderful thought. Then another consideration presented itself, and some of the eagerness faded from his face. For instance, what would his father say when he learned the news? Matthew Sanchez Solano was mayor of Montilla, a good Christian man, one whose home was always open to the sick and needy—and yet it was very possible that he might be disappointed because his son had no wish to pursue a worldly career. After all, Francis had done well with his school work. He had the makings of a good lawyer, possibly even of a doctor or a professor.

"Oh, but he *must* understand!" thought the boy. "I'm just not called to have a career in the world. God wants me for His own service."

Concern for his father's opinion gave way, however, as Francis realized that at least his mother would be pleased about his vocation. For years she had been devoted to the Franciscan Order. Before his birth she had recommended him to the care and protection of the Poor Man of Assisi. Indeed, the very fact that he now bore the name of Francis was due to his mother's love of the saint.

"She'll help me," the boy told himself. "She'll make Father understand. I know it!"

Absorbed in his thoughts, the young student walked slowly homeward, scarcely noticing the fresh beauty of the country landscape. God willing, in a few weeks' time he would ask for the Franciscan habit. He was seventeen years old, in good health, and since childhood he had longed to be a priest—facts which spoke well for his being accepted as a novice. Of course it was true that he had also thought of entering the Society of Jesus. His teachers at school were Jesuits, and many of them were his close friends. One or two had even suggested that he teach a while at the college, then enter the Society. But in the end the thought had always persisted that he was not meant to serve God as a Jesuit teacher. He was meant to work out his salvation as a Franciscan friar.

There were two reasons for this. First, the poverty of the Franciscan Order appealed to him espe-

cially. How fine it was to have nothing of one's own,
to rely upon God's Providence for the very necessi-
ties of life! Then again there was the possibility of
going to Africa as a missionary. For a long time now
the Franciscans had been connected with this
work. Almost every year a little group of friars left
home and family to labor among the bloodthirsty
Moors.

"That's what I'd like best," Francis told himself
as he walked along, "to be a missionary priest in
Africa." Then he smiled at his own words. What
was he saying? If he became a Franciscan, no one
would be concerned with what he *liked.* The
superiors would give him the work *they* thought he
was fitted to do. That was all he had to remember.
And after all, wasn't that the best way of fulfilling
God's Will?

As he was considering this, the clamor of voices
raised in anger suddenly struck his ears from a field
close by.

"Oh! So I'm a coward, am I?" There was a curse,
followed by a groan.

The boy stopped short and looked quickly in the
direction from which the sounds had come. There
he saw two men, armed with swords, about to rush
at each other. One of them was staggering, while
blood streamed down his cheek. Instantly Francis
broke into a run.

"Gentlemen! Gentlemen! In God's Name, stop!"

As he bounded over a low stone wall and into
the field, the wounded man, startled, let his sword
slip from his grasp.

"Curse you, boy!" he gasped hoarsely.

His opponent mocked him. "Coward! The boy came just in time!"

Rage gave the wounded man a renewal of strength, but as he lunged to retrieve his sword, Francis put his foot on it.

"Gentlemen," he said calmly, "fighting is all right if there's good reason for it, but duelling is nothing but murder. What can either of you hope to gain, whichever wins?"

The two enemies glared in astonishment. Then the younger found his voice.

"Be off with you, boy!" he cried, choking with anger. "This is no concern of yours!"

"But I think it is, sir." There was a flicker of laughter in his eyes.

"Why, you, you—who the deuce are you?"

Francis smiled broadly. "I am Francis Solano, and my father is the mayor of Montilla."

For a long moment the would-be combatants stared at the mayor's son, puzzled by the effect which the understanding smile of this mere boy was having upon them. He was unusual. Although his clothes were of fine material and he spoke as the educated son of a good family, there was nothing soft or weak about him. Unquestionably he was quite fearless.

Suddenly the younger man rattled his sword impatiently. "Well, do we fight or don't we? It's getting late."

Francis hesitated. The older man had a deep gash on his head which was bleeding badly. There was no doubt that in a little while, unless something was done, he would die from loss of blood.

"I think this friend of ours needs help," Francis said quickly. "He should go to bed at once."

At these words the wounded man uttered a harsh laugh. "What are you saying, boy? Bed! I'm a stranger in these parts and well-nigh penniless."

"You mean you haven't a place to stay tonight?"

"That's right. But what does it matter? I'm sick of the company of men...of wretches like this one here...and if you'd only give me back my sword..."

"And you?" asked Francis, pretending not to understand and turning quickly to the younger man, "you're a stranger, too?"

"I am. But I could have been at the inn long ago if this blackguard hadn't insulted my honor. Why, he told me right to my face..."

Francis interrupted with a laugh and clapped a hand on the speaker's shoulder. "Let's talk about all this after a good meal at my father's house."

There was a moment's silence. Then the younger man spoke:

"But you said your father was the mayor!"

"That's right."

"Who can go to a mayor's house looking like us?"

Francis laughed again as he bent to pick up the older man's sword. "I have a mother, sirs, who will find great pleasure in looking after all your needs before my father comes. Now, shall we go?"

So it was that the boy and his two companions presently started down the highway leading toward

Montilla. A white handkerchief, pressed into service as a bandage, had stopped the flow of blood from the older man's wound, and he was able to stumble forward weakly under Francis' direction. The little group had gone only a short distance, however, when the sound of a violin fell upon their ears—a gay little melody that told of happy hearts and dancing feet.

Francis looked up eagerly. "That's John the fiddler coming from the fair, friends. Keep your eyes on that bend in the road ahead and I promise you a wonderful sight."

Even as he spoke, the lilting strains grew louder and an elderly vagabond came into view—in tattered green suit and scarlet cloak, his rumpled white hair tumbling to his shoulders. There was an air of such happy abandon about the fiddler that it set Francis' eyes dancing with affectionate merriment.

"He'll pass us by if we're not careful, friends, for his heart is in his song." Then, as the newcomer drew apace: "Oh, John! Haven't you a word for us?"

At once the gay music stopped. "Why, Master Francis! Master Francis Solano! What makes you so late from school?"

"Unexpected business, John. I met two friends a while ago, and now I'm taking them home to dinner. Wouldn't you like to join us?"

The old man drew near and peered curiously at the two strangers. His eyes narrowed as he noted the swords, the white bandage with its ominous red stain, the suspicious scowls that still lingered on both faces. But he smiled and nodded vigorously.

"A good dinner should never be despised, Master Francis. Or new friends. As I've said before, I believe friendship is a foretaste of Heaven, so God bless you for this new chance to enjoy it."

"And you'll play something as we walk?"

"Why not? The time will pass more quickly then."

But even as he lifted his violin to his shoulder, the old man had an idea. "It's been a long time since you played for me, Master Francis. Suppose I help this poor soul with the wound in his head and you make the music?"

Francis smiled. "All right," he said. "Just take his arm, John, and I'll try my luck."

The two enemies exchanged furtive glances as the old fiddler stepped between them. How was it that they had fallen into such unusual company? That the anger which had burned so fiercely within them a short while ago was beginning to subside? But soon came an even greater surprise, for Francis, now a short distance ahead of the little group, had begun to play a melody such as the strangers had never known before. It was a plaintive song, yet one could smile for joy at hearing it.

Puzzled, the wounded man looked at the old fiddler. "What tune is this?" he asked. "And how does a mere boy play so well?"

The latter smiled. "The song, sir, is a hymn to Our Lady. As for the skill of the player. . ."

"*Skill?* But it's more than that!" broke in the younger man. "Why, I'll wager the lad has forgotten

FRANCIS HAD BEGUN TO PLAY
A STRANGE MELODY.

all about us, now that he holds a fiddle in his hands!"

Three pairs of eyes looked down the road to where Francis walked alone. The rays of the setting sun were full upon him as he played and sang, and suddenly tears started in the eyes of the old fiddler.

"I taught the lad to play," he whispered.

"*You?*"

"Yes, through God's mercy. And don't worry that the boy has forgotten you, sirs. This song he sings to Our Lady is offered in both your names."

The recent enemies looked at each other in astonishment. "*What?*"

"That's right, sirs. Master Francis knows many songs, but his favorite is this one—to the Queen of Peace."

CHAPTER 2

FRIAR JOHN'S TEMPTATION

ALAS FOR Francis' hopes to enter the religious life within a few weeks! Because he had done so well with his studies, it was decided that he ought to complete the entire course offered at the Jesuit college in Montilla. It would take three more years, but what of it? A good education never hurt anyone.

In spite of himself, the boy was bitterly disappointed at the delay. Since childhood he had prayed for the grace to be a priest, to consecrate himself to God's service as a Franciscan friar. If the thought sometimes occurred that there might be obstacles, he had always been able to dismiss it. After all, what was most likely to hinder his beloved scheme? Wasn't it the fact that he was the mayor's son? That his father was proud of his abilities and wished him to have a career in the world? Of course! And this had never disturbed him too much, since he knew that his mother was on his side. She would overcome his father's objections.

Now, however, Francis was really worried. His

vocation was being tested in such an unexpected manner!

"Maybe the friars don't want me after all," he thought, "and this business of continuing my education is only an excuse. Perhaps Father Guardian thinks I wouldn't persevere. Oh, but that's not so! I'd do my very best to keep the rule. I'd pray. . .and study. . .and work. . .I'd do *anything*, no matter how hard!"

Father Peter de Ojeda, the Novice Master at the friary, was fully aware of his young friend's disappointment. In most instances he would have said that a youth who showed as strong an attraction for the religious life as did Francis, who was so genuinely anxious to fashion himself into another Christ, ought to be received into the community at once. A religious vocation is very precious. It deserves encouragement and protection. And even then, Father Peter reflected sadly, the Devil often succeeds in drawing young souls from the way God means them to go.

"But no one seems to fear for me," said Francis one day as the two walked together in the friary garden. "Oh, Father! Why must I be a simple lay student at the Jesuit college when I could follow the same studies here as a friar?"

The priest smiled. "My son, let me ask you something."

"Yes, Father?"

"What is a saint?"

The boy's dark eyes searched those of his companion curiously. "A saint? Why, one who loves God and does His Will."

"That's right, Francis. But you speak these words so glibly. Let me hear them again. Yes—and this time pretend that I'm a poor savage who has come to you for instruction. I've heard about the Christian religion and am anxious to be baptized. I know that when the Sacrament of Baptism is bestowed upon me, my soul will be made pure and clean. But I also know that through the passing years many Christians lose their baptismal innocence. I don't want to be one of these, Francis. I want to remain God's friend. I want to be a saint. Now—how am I going to do this?"

It was several minutes before the boy chanced upon one explanation which interested the "savage" before him. A saint, he said, is a person who has made himself God's tool. He does the work which duty sets before him. He does not concern himself as to whether or not he likes this work— whether he would have chosen it for himself if free to do so. He merely does it as well as he can. When circumstances put an end to activity, he does not fret. He is still God's tool—broken, of course, but through no fault of his own. If in time he is mended, well and good. If not, well and good also.

"I could add to your description of a saint," said Father Peter, "but on the whole it's a fair one. Now, be quiet a moment and give me another."

There was silence in the garden. From time to time the friar cast an amused glance at the young student beside him. That wrinkled brow, those half-shut eyes! Ah, yes—Francis Solano was really thinking hard—and quite unaware that he was about to do himself a great good.

Suddenly the boy looked up. "I've another definition of a saint now, Father. And maybe it's better suited to the poor savage than the first."

"Well, what is it?"

"A saint is a chalice."

"*What?*"

"A saint has emptied his heart of earthly things, so that it may hold Christ. Therefore, he has made himself like a chalice. And having done this, he has no will but Christ's Will within him—which is the Will of God the Father."

The friar laughed, so heartily that the boy never guessed the genuine admiration his words had aroused. "You credit our poor savage with considerable intelligence, Francis. Do you think he'll understand this talk of tools and chalices and emptied hearts?"

A flush crept over the young man's face. "Perhaps not. Perhaps I don't make things too clear. But how I wish I could! You see, something tells me that there can be great peace in the emptied heart."

Father Peter, whose work as Novice Master had given him a true understanding of men's souls, laughed again. "Fine words, my son. What a pity that you don't believe them."

Francis stared. *"Don't believe them?"*

"That's right. You speak the truth when you say that the heart must be emptied of earthly things before it can be a saint's heart—a chalice to hold Christ, our true Peace. But you have no emptied

A SAINT HAS EMPTIED HIS HEART SO
THAT IT MAY HOLD CHRIST.

heart, young friend, when you complain about the
delay in being accepted at the friary. Your will is
still very much in evidence."

"But Father! I wasn't talking about myself! I was
just giving you a description of a saint!"

"And there's a difference?"

Francis was silent before the friar's kindly gaze,
realizing that he had just discovered a disturbing
truth. Finally he spoke:

"There's a very great difference."

"All right. And what are you doing about it?"

"Why, nothing...at least, I haven't really
thought about it..."

"Listen, my son. A while ago you gave me a very
beautiful description of a saint—a person who has
emptied his heart of earthly desires and made it
into a chalice to hold Christ. Now, who is given the
grace to do this...this *emptying?*"

The boy hesitated. "I suppose many people have
the grace, Father."

"*Many people?* God gives this grace to us all,
Francis! Isn't it wonderful?"

There was another moment's silence. Then
Francis smiled wryly. "Yes, Father. But it's so easy
to forget...to have ideas and plans of one's
own...to be discouraged because they don't work
out..."

Father Peter nodded. "I know, my son. But as
you yourself have said, there is great peace in the
emptied heart. So why not try a new kind of living
for the next three years?"

"You mean...?"

"I mean with your heart emptied of its own desires and become a chalice to hold Christ. Oh, Francis! When you open your heart to Him living within you, it will be so much easier than you think to do the Will of the Heavenly Father!"

The Novice Master was right, and the three years of higher studies which Francis had dreaded passed more fruitfully than he had dared to hope. Then in 1569, when he was twenty years old, came the day he had dreamed of for so long. He was accepted as a novice by the Franciscan friars in Montilla—those men who followed the rule of life laid down by Saint Peter of Alcantara a few years previous. Now he was no longer the mayor's son, a youth who led his classes at the Jesuit college, who could coax a sad or merry tune from the most ordinary violin. No, he was a member of the Alcantrine Franciscans—the most austere religious Order in Spain. He was Friar Francis Solano, a tool of God, a chalice for Christ.

As he received the grey woolen habit from the hands of the Father Provincial, Friar Francis could hardly restrain his joy. At last his patience was being rewarded! And there was even more happiness to come, for after one year's trial as a novice he would be permitted to make his religious profession—the vows which would bind him to God's special service forever. Then in six more years he would be ready to be ordained a priest.

"The year 1576!" he thought joyfully. "Surely that will be the most wonderful year in my whole life?"

But if Francis was at peace, truly happy in the grey habit of the Order he loved with the white cord about his waist, there was another young man who was not. This was Friar John, who had come to the novitiate with the same eagerness as Francis, who had desired to be a priest, to go some day as a missionary to foreign lands, but who now found himself strangely repelled by the religious life—the prayers. . .the fasts. . .the obedience required of him in the smallest matters. . .surely he could not persevere for long in such a drab existence.

"I don't understand what's happened," he told Francis one day. "All of a sudden I want to run away from here, back to my old life in the world with its comforts and pleasures. Oh, my brother! What's wrong with me that I no longer want to be a priest?"

Francis was a little embarrassed. This was plainly a problem for the Novice Master to decide, not for a fellow-beginner in the religious life. But Friar John shook his head at the objection.

"Father Peter told me to come to you," he declared emphatically. "I explained everything to him this morning, believing he could help me. But he gave me almost no encouragement. Then, just as I was leaving his cell, he smiled in the most peculiar fashion. 'Go and talk to Friar Francis,' he said. 'Ask him for his definition of a saint.'"

Francis could hardly believe his ears. Surely there must be some mistake. Surely Friar John was joking. Yet one glance at the latter's serious face convinced him this was not so. Friar John really had a problem—and he was really anxious to solve it.

"In God's Name I beg you, tell me what strange definition you have for a saint!" he urged. "Maybe it will bring me peace."

Reluctantly Francis set himself to describe the saint's heart—that heart which has emptied itself of every personal desire and become a chalice to hold Christ. His words came slowly at first, for he was still embarrassed that such a holy man as Father Peter de Ojeda had sent this fellow-novice for comfort and advice. But presently he had lost his self-consciousness, and Friar John's eyes widened as he listened to the fervent words.

"It was because I wanted to give myself to God in a really complete way that I came here to the friary," he said. "And so it was with you, Friar John. Both of us know that there are millions of good people out in the world. . .that it is possible to do a wonderful work for God without going into religion. But God chose us for something more, and so we decided to pray and suffer in a friary. This seemed the best way for us."

"Yes, but I don't feel that way any longer. Why, I've come to despise suffering, Friar Francis! And if I have to pray any more . . . or read pious books. . ."

"Then your heart isn't emptied, Friar John. It's no longer a chalice to hold Christ. What's happened? What do you want to do?"

The young man hesitated. Surely Friar Francis would be scandalized if he knew the truth! And yet he must know it some time. . .

"I want to go to the New World!" he burst out.
"I want some adventure and excitement. Yes, and
wealth. Oh, Friar Francis, it's true that when I first
came here I dreamed of being a saint...a worthy
priest. But it's too hard, I tell you. I'm not meant
for such a life. And these days when so many are
going to Peru...when men can become wealthy
overnight with the gold they find in the Andes..."

Francis stared unbelievingly. Since childhood he
had known that the Devil is an angel, with an
angel's keen intelligence, and that he is ever on the
lookout for souls. But not until now had he felt the
evil presence so strongly.

CHAPTER 3

THE SECRET

THE NOVICE Master was not surprised when Friar John came to him later in the day and announced that he still wished to leave the friary. Yes—Friar Francis had spoken long and earnestly to him, had encouraged him to empty his heart of worldly desires and make it into a chalice to hold Christ. But this counsel, wise and true as he knew it to be, he did not feel strong enough to accept. There was still the burning desire to escape from the restraining walls of the friary, to go to Peru and seek his fortune in the gold and silver mines.

The priest was quiet. "Then go, my son," he said, his hand raised in blessing. "And may you do a good work for God as a layman."

Although the Novice Master was calm over Friar John's departure, it was different with Francis. When he discovered that his fellow-novice had gone back to the world, that he would be sailing for America in a week's time, his heart was heavy.

"Oh, Father Peter! How dreadful I couldn't help

him! What's going to become of John now?"

"Why, I guess he'll be like any other young adventurer. He'll bend all his energies to getting ahead in the New World. His friends will be chosen from the rich and powerful. He'll convince himself that there's nothing desirable in suffering or poverty. . ."

"If I had just prayed a little harder when I was talking to him!"

The Novice Master shook his head. "No, don't blame yourself. I've seen dozens of young men turn away from the religious life, and some had gone much further than Friar John. They weren't bad boys, either. Just weak. Every day I remember them at the Holy Sacrifice of the Mass—that in the end God will see fit to bless their weakness and make them His true servants."

Francis hesitated. "I'd like to remember John," he said hopefully, "to pray that he be given a special grace."

"Yes? And what's that?"

"That he come back to us some day, Father; that he may go to God wearing the habit of our Order."

Francis' sincerity touched the Novice Master deeply, and he readily blessed his intention. "It's a splendid idea," he said. "Don't forget it, my son."

Francis did not forget. As time passed, he often thought of Friar John—especially on his own Profession Day, April 25, 1570, when he made the complete offering of his body and soul to God.

"I'm sure John's not interested in religion any more," he told himself sadly. "And probably he never even thinks of me. But I'll pray for him until I die. Dear Lord, won't You please hear me? Won't You please give John the grace to come back to Your service some day?"

The Franciscan friary at Montilla was a small and overcrowded building, and three years after Francis' profession the Father Guardian announced that he was sending a few of the younger religious to another house of the Order. This friary was near Seville, and was dedicated to Our Lady of Loreto. It would be their home for an indefinite period.

"You'll follow the usual studies for Ordination," he told the little group. "Logic, philosophy, Scriptures. And I warn you that this house at Loreto isn't too comfortable. It's hot in the summer and cold in the winter. The cells are small, and many are in need of repairs that we can't afford. But don't worry. It seems that those who persevere at Loreto always profit from these hardships. They attain to a surprising love for suffering—finding it to be the best coin with which to ransom sinners. And what is the result of all this? Why, many of our friars, young men like yourselves, have become saints!"

Francis was delighted when he learned that he was among those being sent to Loreto—even though this meant that he would not be able to see his family as frequently as in the past. Nor did his feelings change when it was discovered, shortly after his arrival, that there was no cell available for his use.

"We'll have to find some kind of a room for you," said the Father Guardian in a worried voice. "But where? We're terribly overcrowded."

Even as he spoke, the bell in the church tower began to ring for Vespers. Francis looked toward the sounding bronze.

"Does anybody live up there, Father Guardian?"

The superior turned to where Francis was pointing. "In the church tower? Of course not! That would hardly do for a cell, Friar Francis. The wind and rain come in from all sides."

"If a little shelter could be built, there wouldn't be too much trouble from the wind and rain. Oh, Father Guardian! Won't you please give permission for this? I'd be so happy to have a cell above the church!"

The Father Guardian felt sure that the newcomer would regret his wish to live in a drafty tower, but finally he gave the desired permission. By sundown a small wooden house had been erected beneath the church bell, and that night Francis found himself established in his lofty quarters.

Before he went to bed, the young religious looked out at the vast dome of the sky, glowing now with a myriad of stars, and his heart swelled with happiness. This peace, this overpowering beauty before him, were but shadows of Heaven—the smallest hints of the good things which God has in store for those who serve Him faithfully. And as he reflected upon this, Francis turned impulsively toward the church below, to the darkened sanctuary where the Creator of all this beauty lay hidden under the guise of a piece of bread. Quietly he offered a familiar prayer:

THAT NIGHT FRANCIS FOUND HIMSELF
ESTABLISHED IN HIS LOFTY QUARTERS.

"We adore Thee, O Lord Jesus Christ, here
and in all the churches of the whole world; and
we bless Thee, because by Thy holy cross Thou
didst redeem the world."

Three years passed at Loreto—the final period
of preparation for the priesthood. Francis prayed
and studied and worked, always offering himself
and his actions to the Eternal Father in union with
Christ's death upon Calvary—particularly at Holy
Mass, for he knew that this is the best prayer a
human being can offer.

One September afternoon in the year 1576, a
young lay Brother mounted the winding stairway to
Francis' tower cell. Although he was a newcomer
to Loreto, and the least educated of any in the
entire community, Brother Joseph had already discovered life's most important truth: that each person in the world, whether rich or poor, wise or
stupid, has a similar task to perform. *Using the
graces God gives him, he is expected to save his soul
and become a saint.*

Now Brother Joseph was convinced that he
might become a saint more readily if he were
allowed to speak with Friar Francis Solano from
time to time, and so that morning he had
approached the Novice Master for the necessary
permission.

"Yes, you may spend fifteen minutes with Friar
Francis," the latter had told him, smiling. "But be
sure to pay your visit after Vespers. By that time
our good friend will have finished his classes and

most of his studying. You see, Brother Joseph, he's very busy these days. Of course you know why?"

The lay Brother had nodded vigorously. "Oh, yes, Father! He's to be ordained a priest in two weeks. But don't worry that I'll tire him. I'll come back to the kitchen as soon as my fifteen minutes are up."

Now, as he mounted the tower stairs, Brother Joseph's face reflected his satisfaction. "There's something different about Friar Francis Solano," he told himself. "Yesterday as we were assisting at Father Guardian's Mass, I happened to look across at him. Why, his face was the happiest I've ever seen! It was almost shining! I knew then that this young man hears Mass as does no one else in the friary; that he has some wonderful secret with God. Oh, I wonder if he would tell me what it is?"

With this, the lay Brother reached the top of the stairs and knocked on Francis' door. The young friar was praying, and he came to himself slowly. He was tired after a long day in the classroom, and had been looking forward to spending his free hour alone. But there was a smile on his lips as he arose and went to open the door. The Heavenly Father was so good! He was sending another little trial—a sacrifice, which in a few short hours. . .

"Why, Brother Joseph! Come in!"

The latter bowed, and stepped quickly inside the little wooden shelter. "I won't keep you long, Friar Francis. I just came to ask one question. If you can answer it fully, I'll be most grateful."

The young religious nodded encouragingly. "And

what's your question? Believe me, I'll do my best
to answer it."

Brother Joseph did not hesitate. "I want to know
how to hear Mass," he said simply.

Then, as Francis stared in amazement: "Of
course I'm always attentive in church. I ask God
for different blessings, for myself and for others. I
say the Rosary or other prayers while the priest
offers the Holy Sacrifice. But there seems to be
something missing. I. . .I can never feel satisfied
that I've done all that God expected me to do. Why
is this, Friar Francis? What have I forgotten?"

For a moment it was very quiet in the little cell,
and Brother Joseph had a sudden and disturbing
thought. Friar Francis was looking at him so
strangely, his eyes glowing and distant. Could it be
that he was angry? That he believed an ignorant
lay Brother had no business asking questions about
the Mass but should be satisfied with imitating the
other lay Brothers—doing his work well, saying
what prayers the Rule prescribed, then keeping
silence unless spoken to by a superior?

Overcome with confusion, Brother Joseph slowly
began to retreat, his eyes lowered and deep color
in his cheeks. "I didn't mean to set myself up as
important," he whispered. "Friar Francis, please
believe that all my life I've wanted to know how
to pray properly. . .and when I saw you at Mass
yesterday, so happy, so filled with peace. . ."

Suddenly he stopped. Friar Francis was at his
side, holding the door so that he could not open
it! And he was smiling!

"Don't go, Brother. And forgive me for my silence. It was just that...well, I was a little frightened."

Brother Joseph stared. "Frightened? *Of me?*"

"No. And 'frightened' isn't the right word, Brother. I was thinking of the goodness of the Eternal Father, and one can never be frightened by that. Let's say, rather, that I was overcome when you spoke about the Holy Sacrifice."

Brother Joseph nodded, although he was not quite sure what his companion meant. "I've a few minutes of free time," he began humbly. "If you could tell me a little something about the Mass. . ."

Francis led his visitor to a small stool near the window. "Of course," he said. "Sit down, Brother."

During the next five minutes Brother Joseph learned more about the Holy Sacrifice than he had ever dreamed possible. He discovered that he was meant to go through life as Christ had done, his will ever united to that of the Heavenly Father. Naturally this meant accepting pain and disappointment in a cheerful spirit, something that is far from easy, since these things are against nature and very rarely show themselves as blessings. But such a sacrifice was expected of all who would gain Heaven.

"For Christ, the Will of the Eternal Father was that He should be obedient unto the death of the Cross," explained Francis. "For us, it is much the same thing."

Brother Joseph shivered, while a puzzled look crept into his eyes. "I know that Christ was crucified on Calvary," he said slowly. "But surely the

Heavenly Father doesn't mean...why, it's impossible that we should all be crucified, too!"

Francis spoke gently: "Our *wills* must be crucified, Brother Joseph. And though suffering has no merit of itself, when we unite it to Christ's suffering its value becomes very great indeed. Therefore, each morning at Mass, when the priest offers Our Lord to the Eternal Father, we must not be mere onlookers. At that great moment we must join in offering Him to the Father. Then, we must offer ourselves, too—the little pains and troubles we've endured since our last Mass, the joys and happiness that have come our way—above all, our *wills*. And this is to be done cheerfully, Brother Joseph, else we lose much merit. Yes, we must offer ourselves to do the Will of the Heavenly Father with the same eagerness with which Our Lord offered Himself for the redemption of sinners. Our hearts must be emptied of self-love only to be filled again to overflowing with the love of God and our neighbor."

Brother Joseph shook his head. "It sounds very hard."

"Hard? Sensible, rather. If the Heavenly Father has created us out of nothing, if He has prepared for us an everlasting happiness in Heaven, what is so unusual about our wishing to please Him, to do His Will? Because until we learn to make our wills like His, we cannot enter Heaven."

The words were serious ones, but spoken in such a kindly way that Brother Joseph took heart. So— he was meant to give himself completely to the Heavenly Father? To crucify his will and become a little victim in union with Christ, the all-holy Victim, at every Mass?

"I'll try very hard to remember what you've told me," he said slowly. "Tomorrow morning, at the Offertory of the Mass, I'll make a real effort to give myself, my *whole* self, to the Eternal Father. Oh, Friar Francis! Please pray for me that I don't weaken!"

Friar Francis laughed. "You're making holiness too hard," he said. "Brother Joseph, it's true that we must give up our wills to the Heavenly Father, as Christ did, if we really wish to please Him. But that's just part of the story."

"Yes? What else?"

"When the Eternal Father sees the holy Gift that is being offered to Him—His own crucified Son offering Himself (with us offering Him, too, and also offering our little selves), He will never refuse to accept It. We have won His Heart by this holy Offering, and He is open to give us anything we ask for in return—anything that is good for us, of course."

"Oh, that sounds wonderful!" exclaimed Brother Joseph.

"And the better we have offered up ourselves, our wills," continued Friar Francis, "the more the Heavenly Father will hear us. So if we assist at Mass with a true spirit of sacrifice, our prayers will become all-powerful with the Heavenly Father. Joined with Our Lord's offering of Himself, we will prevail upon Him to grant all our petitions— especially petitions for holy things."

"Oh, Friar Francis!" exclaimed Brother Joseph with a gulp. "That sounds wonderful," he repeated. "And to think how many times I've missed daily Mass before I entered the Order, just because I wanted to do something else instead!"

"I think you're beginning to understand," smiled Friar Francis.

"Missing a Mass is like turning your back on a great Treasure!" added Brother Joseph.

"Yes. And when we follow the Mass to its real climax, when we receive Holy Communion, why, there's still more, Brother Joseph. Then the Eternal Father gives us Christ to live in our souls, to take with us to our work, so that gradually our wills may become like His and we may make an even better offering at our next Mass, receiving even more holy gifts from the Heavenly Father."

For a long moment Brother Joseph was silent, his eyes filled with reverence. So, he had been right! Friar Francis did have a secret . . . a most wonderful secret . . .

CHAPTER 4

MICHAEL FACES DEATH

IN TWO WEEKS' time the day for which Francis had waited and prayed so faithfully arrived. With a few companions he was ordained a priest. From now on his would be the wonderful power to take ordinary bread and wine and turn them into the Body and Blood of Christ. And his, too, would be the power to cleanse souls from sin, to administer the mysterious and strengthening grace which God has ready for everyone who kneels in Confession.

"How wonderful!" the young man thought. "Oh, dear Lord, please let me use these gifts properly! And please let me go to Africa very soon as a missionary. . ."

Yes, the old desire which had filled his heart as a boy still remained with Francis. Although he loved the orderly life at Our Lady of Loreto, the peace and quiet of his tower cell, the young priest could not help but think of the many millions of Moors in Africa who followed the teachings of Mohammed and who considered it a privilege to

kill every Christian they could find! Oh, what a joy
to go to them, to preach and baptize, to substitute
knowledge for ignorance and to show that no man
can be happy as long as he hates and persecutes
even one of his fellows! What did it matter if suffering and martyrdom followed? This would be only
further evidences of God's favor.

At the age of twenty-seven, Father Francis Solano
was well equipped both by nature and training to
be a successful missionary. And with Africa in dire
need of great numbers of priests, what was more
likely than that his superiors should send him to
help those friars who already were hard at work
there? Yet as the weeks passed, the Father Guardian made no move in this direction. Instead, he
gave Francis a totally different kind of work. Until
further notice Francis was to be choir director for
the friary. He was to have full charge of the sacred
music, instructing his fellow-religious how to chant
the Divine Office and sing the High Mass.

"You have a natural talent for music," declared
the older friar. "You play the violin well, and your
voice is good, too. I think you'll do very nicely with
this new work."

"I'll try, Father Guardian," Francis said cheerfully. "I'll try very hard."

So it was that the priests, and even the lay
Brothers, assembled each day for their musical
instruction under Francis. Of course the chanting
of the Divine Office was a work belonging only to
the first group, but the new choir director felt that
it would do no harm for everyone in the community

to assist at the lessons. What matter if the lay Brothers' chief work was to cook, to sweep, to mend, to wash dishes? That many of them scarcely knew how to read, let alone understand the Latin words of the hymns?

"When we sing at Mass, or at any other service, we are really praying," said Francis encouragingly. "And if God hasn't given us a good voice or a quick mind for Latin, it doesn't matter at all. Only this matters: that we learn to use properly what voice and mind we have. In that way we will really glorify God."

Very soon music had taken on a fresh importance for the community, and the men and women of the countryside, impressed by the hearty singing of the friars, finally ventured to join their own voices in singing the more familiar chants at Sunday Mass. When some months had passed, the Father Guardian called Francis to his cell.

"My son, you're doing a splendid work," he said approvingly. "We've never had such fine singing here before."

Of course Francis was happy at these words. Yet there were still times when he thought longingly of the African missions. How fine it would be to sing God's praises there! However, he did not cling to this desire. Obedience, the first rule of the religious life, was still his whole concern. Just now it seemed as if God was quite satisfied that he was trying to be a good choir director.

"And that's all that matters," Francis told himself, "that God is served."

Two years passed, and suddenly the quiet days at Loreto came to an end. Francis' father was called home to God. Since Francis' mother was in poor health, with her eyesight failing, it was thought best that Francis should go to her. He could live in the friary at Montilla, that beloved spot where he had first put on the Franciscan habit nine years before.

The young religious was pleasantly surprised by the new assignment. Yet when the time for leavetaking came, he experienced a keen sorrow. Many of his close friends in Loreto were advanced in years, and it seemed unlikely that he would ever see them again in this world. Old Brother Philip, for instance, who worked in the kitchen, and whose love of God was so great that he was constantly singing His praises. Off key, of course, and frequently when the Rule prescribed complete silence in the house, but with such a childlike simplicity that generally the fault was overlooked. There was also lame Brother Andrew, whose life was one long and beautiful prayer.

"I have to go slowly when I walk," he had confided once to Francis. "Thus, I have plenty of time at each step to tell Our Lord that I love Him."

There were Father Guardian and the Father Vicar, too—both saints. And the others whom Francis had taught to know and love the music of the Church and whom he had come to love like brothers. Oh, how he would miss all these friends and his work with them!

Yet, safely arrived in Montilla, the young priest was soon possessed of his usual inner peace. More than ever now he realized that in doing the will of his superiors he was truly doing the Will of God. What matter if he never left Spain as a missionary? That others experienced the great joy of converting and baptizing the Moors? He would share in the work in another fashion. Every day he would offer prayers and sacrifices for the spread of Christ's Kingdom in Africa.

In Montilla, where he had been born twenty-nine years before, Francis soon settled down to the familiar and peaceful life of the friary. At midnight he and his fellow-religious arose to chant Matins and Lauds, the official prayer whereby the Church as a body gives praise to God. Later in the morning came a return to the parish church for Prime and Terce, the Hours of the Divine Office which follow Matins and Lauds. However, all this was but a preparation for the most important function of the day—the Conventual Mass, at which the entire community assisted. Afterwards, at various altars in the friary, each priest offered his private Mass.

In Montilla, Francis once more had the opportunity to put his musical talents to use, for even as at Loreto, he was given the task of training the community in singing. At the organ, or in his regular place with the brethren, he daily raised his splendid voice in praise of God.

"We've never had such a fine musician as Father Francis," declared the younger friars. "Surely if he had stayed in the world he would have made a great name for himself."

Some of the older friars smiled. They felt quite sure that Francis would still make a great name for himself—not as a musician, of course, but in a far more important capacity.

"He's a saint," old Father Matthew announced emphatically. "Wait and see if God doesn't prove it's so by letting him work a miracle."

The eyes of all widened. A *miracle?* And by one of their own religious? How wonderful!

"What do you suppose it will be?" asked Brother Bartholomew excitedly. "A cure, maybe? Or the raising to life of a dead person?"

Father Matthew shook his head. "Who knows? But I'm sure of one thing, my son. When the miracle does occur, it will bring great joy to everyone here. It will show that Montilla is the birthplace of a true hero, and our friary his home."

Brother Bartholomew had a second question. "Do you suppose it will happen soon, Father?"

The old priest smiled, then nodded slowly. "Yes," he said, "I'm pretty sure it will."

Father Matthew was right. Just a few days later, as Francis was setting out one morning on a begging trip through the town, a man came running after him. He was Diego Lopez, a well-to-do merchant, known throughout Montilla for his cheerful smile and ready wit. But today there were tears in Diego's eyes, and the strained and anxious look on his pale face showed that recently he had spent many a sleepless night.

"Father, it's my little boy!" he gasped, his hands clasping and unclasping nervously. "We've prayed and prayed for Michael, but the doctor says he's going to die. Oh, if you could just stop by for a moment..."

An expression of concern crossed Francis' face. Surely eleven-year-old Michael Lopez was a husky lad? Why, just recently he had seen him playing ball with other boys at the Jesuit college...and playing very well, too.

"Michael's been sick for two weeks, Father," put in Diego quickly. "An infection of some sort. Yesterday he had the Last Rites from Father Anthony. But his grandmother insists that if you'll come and say a prayer or two..."

Francis hesitated. The food supply at the friary was running low, and only an hour ago he had asked the Father Guardian for permission to go begging in the town. Now, if he went with Diego, his well-laid plans for visiting a number of wealthy families would have to be set aside. There would scarcely be enough for the friars' noonday meal. Yet seeing the stricken look on Diego's face, he dismissed this objection. To comfort and encourage a suffering soul is always a holy work, no matter what inconvenience it may cause. As for the empty larder in the friary—well, he knew that his fellow-religious would not mind going hungry under such circumstances. And Father Guardian would surely want him to go with Diego.

Quickly he turned to the anxious Diego. "Of course I'll come," he said. "From what I saw of him the other day, your Michael is a fine boy."

The man choked back a great sob. "He...he's

our only child, Father! I don't know what we'll do if anything happens to him!"

Francis smiled again, shifted his empty basket from one arm to the other, and indicated that he was ready to go. Well he knew that of himself he could do nothing for young Michael. Yet God hears every prayer, and so even now he was asking that His peace descend upon the troubled household, even if not through the lad's recovery. He was asking for them the grace for which the Lopez family had perhaps never asked in their whole lives—the grace of being completely united to God's Will.

There were many people about Diego's home when he and Francis arrived—friends, servants, relatives. All made way for the pair, kneeling for a blessing from the grey-habited priest. Then suddenly there was a commotion, and a young woman, her eyes red from weeping, pressed forward. It was Maria Lopez, Michael's mother.

"Oh, Father! Thank God you've come!"

Francis set down his basket. "Yes, I've come," he said gently. "Where is the little one?"

Maria pointed to a heavily carved door down the hall, then broke into sobs. "In there," she choked. "Oh, my poor little boy! The doctor says he's going to die today..."

Preceded by Diego and Maria, Francis went quickly down the passageway into the sickroom. It was a beautifully furnished chamber overlooking a rose garden. Sunlight streamed through the windows onto the thick Persian carpets, the tables and chairs of rare mahogany, but the newcomer had no eyes for these. Instead, he hastened toward the huge canopied bed in one corner and bent over the small figure half hidden within its depths.

"Michael, it's Father Francis," he whispered, smiling. "I've come to see you."

There was no answer. Indeed, the eleven-year-old boy gave no sign that he had heard the priest's greeting. His eyes were closed, and his face, covered with hideous ulcers, was almost green in color. From time to time he gave a great gasp as he fought for breath.

Francis looked anxiously toward the doctor, but the latter shook his head. "The lad can't last more than a few hours, Father," he murmured. "Here— just look at this."

In spite of himself, the young priest uttered a cry of dismay as the doctor pulled back the covers. Why, poor little Michael's body was a mass of running sores which not even the thick bandages could conceal! Surely, in such a condition. . .

The doctor read his thoughts. "Yes, Father. The poison is affecting his heart. And there's nothing that anyone can do about it."

At these words, Maria Lopez threw herself on her knees beside the bed. "No! No!" she moaned. "Michael can't die! He's all I have. . .he's my only child. . ."

Suddenly Diego picked up a well-worn book from a nearby table and hurried to Francis' side. "The lad's grandmother is ill herself, Father, but she did say that if you would read one of the Gospels over Michael. . .just any one. . .God would

HE BEGAN TO READ FROM ST. JOHN'S GOSPEL.

hear your prayers and leave the boy with us. Will you? Please?"

Slowly Francis took the book which Diego handed to him, made the Sign of the Cross and opened it at random. Then in reverent tones he began to read the words of Saint John upon which he had chanced. And as he read, a hush fell upon the room. Maria's sobs ceased and a faint ray of hope appeared in her tearful eyes. For Francis, inspired by the Holy Spirit, was reading the stirring words from the fourth chapter of Saint John's Gospel:

"And there was a certain ruler, whose son was sick at Capharnaum. He, having heard that Jesus was come from Judea into Galilee, went to Him and prayed Him to come down and heal his son, for he was at the point of death. Jesus, therefore, said to him: Unless you see signs and wonders, you believe not. The ruler said to Him: Lord, come down before my son dies. Jesus said to him: Go your way, your son lives. The man believed the words which Jesus said to him, and went his way. And as he was going down, his servants met him. And they brought word, saying that his son lived. He asked therefore of them the hour wherein he grew better. And they said to him: Yesterday at the seventh hour the fever left him. The father therefore knew that it was at the same hour that Jesus said to him: Your son lives. And himself believed, and his whole house. . ."

CHAPTER 5

THE FATHER

BEFORE THE day was over, all Montilla was in a state of great excitement. Eleven-year-old Michael Lopez was not going to die after all! The dreadful ulcers which had covered his whole body for two weeks were drying up. No longer had he a fever. He was crying out for food—and this, after not having taken any nourishment for several days. .

"It's good Father Francis who's responsible!" Maria Lopez insisted joyfully when unbelieving friends and neighbors flocked to the house. "Oh, God be praised for sending him to us . . ."

"He's the most wonderful man I ever met!" cried Diego. "As long as I live, I'll never forget the way in which he read those holy words from the Gospel . . ."

"Didn't I tell you that my plan would work?" exclaimed his mother-in-law. (She also was beginning to feel much beter.) "Father Francis' prayers have true power with God."

The Franciscan friars in Montilla were just as

elated over the miracle as the townsfolk, particularly old Father Matthew. Hadn't he always known that Francis was a great soul? Hadn't he even prophesied that there would be a miracle to prove it? And as other wonders began to be credited to Francis' prayers—the cure of a beggar suffering from a variety of ailments, the settling of longstanding disputes between this family and that, the conversion of half a dozen hardened sinners—the old man's pulse quickened with joy. Just one thing was cause for sadness—the knowledge that soon Francis would be leaving his native town. Worried about the honors which now were being heaped upon him, he had applied for a transfer to some other house of the Order. Oddly enough, his request had been granted at once. In a few days he was to go to Arizafa, where he would fill the post of Novice Master.

Although their hearts were heavy at the impending loss, Father Matthew and the others of the community realized the wisdom behind the Father Provincial's unexpected order. The friary in Arizafa was larger than the one in Montilla, and there was a considerable number of novices there. With Father Francis as their instructor, these young men would have the inestimable advantage of seeing how a saint lives and works and prays. Though they themselves might be of no more than average virtue, there was a good chance that under his direction they would become real saints. The result? Someday as priests they would go forth to make others holy, too. They would carry Father Francis' wonderful spirit throughout Spain, even to the faraway missions in Africa. Then thousands of men and women, at present not at all concerned about knowing and loving God, would find themselves asking for, and receiving, the most wonderful graces.

"Truly, one good man can help to change the face of the earth," Father Matthew told himself emphatically. And this thought brought another, the one so often expressed by Mother Teresa of Jesus, the great Carmelite reformer whose monasteries of cloistered nuns were now multiplying so wonderfully throughout Spain:

"One perfect soul can do more for God's glory than a thousand ordinary souls."

Like Father Matthew, Francis was fully aware of Mother Teresa's famous saying, and at Arizafa he lost no time in passing it along to the young men under his care. Well he knew the importance of the task he had been given—the training of young men to be wise and holy priests and religious—and so he let pass no opportunity to accomplish this end. He made use of even the simplest things, such as a rosebush in the friary garden, to illustrate to the novices the manner in which they were to grow in the service of God.

For instance, when the rains fell, or the sun beat down mercilessly, or the pruning knife was used, what could the rosebush do but obey the law of its nature whereby it was passive to the elements and to the intelligence of the human being in charge of its welfare? The result was that eventually the bush brought forth many beautiful and fragrant flowers, delighting those who gazed upon it and turning their thoughts to the Creator of such perfection.

"Why not think of this often?" Francis asked the novices one day when they were out for a walk. "You see, in one way we are plants, too—in God's garden. If we give ourselves completely into His keeping, we cannot help but flourish as He planned."

For a moment there was silence, each of the novices pondering the latest suggestion of the Novice Master. But presently a troubled expression on one young face caused Francis to laugh heartily.

"What's the trouble, Friar Philip? Don't you like the idea of the rain or the sunshine—*or* the pruning knife?"

The youth hesitated. "Yes, Father. They're . . . they're all right, I guess."

"Well, what is it then?"

The novice colored. "I . . .oh, Father! It's so hard to explain!"

By now all eyes were on the young religious, who was shifting awkwardly from one foot to the other. Francis knew full well what was troubling him. Like so many beginners in the spiritual life, Friar Philip had been trying to be a great saint in just a few days, not realizing to what an extent his aspiration was tinged with pride. As a result, he had become disheartened at a seeming lack of progress, and now this talk of rain and sunshine and a pruning knife had even frightened him.

WE ARE PLANTS, TOO—IN GOD'S GARDEN.

"My son, who founded our Order?" Francis asked suddenly.

Taken aback by such a simple question, Friar Philip stared in amazement. "Why, Francis of Assisi," he said slowly, "in the thirteenth century."

"Yes. And for what was our Father Francis noted?"

"Well..."

"He was always joyful, wasn't he?"

"Yes, Father."

The Novice Master reached out a friendly hand. "Little brother, the good man knew all about the rain and the sunshine and the pruning knife—those trials which God has in store for every soul—but he knew about the worth of a smile, too. So perhaps we should try to find out about it also?"

Again there was silence, and after a moment Francis continued with his lesson. In simple words he pointed out that the trials God sends are not easy to bear, even for those who have the light of faith and who are anxious to advance in the way of perfection. Yet they become less painful if one meets them with a smile.

"Just a little smile will do," Francis explained.

"But I don't feel like smiling when I have a trial," objected Friar Philip. "Why, when my head aches, or things don't work out the way I planned, I don't feel a bit happy."

"It's that way with me, too," put in Friar Paul earnestly. "Yesterday, after I was scolded for breaking a dish..."

"You felt quite hurt."

"Yes, Father."

"You didn't smile at all."

"No, Father."

"Well, the next time something unpleasant happens, why not try this plan? That is, say 'Yes' to God with a smile—both inside your heart and on your face. Smile not for yourself, but for Him. If you do this, whatever work you are doing will have much more value before God."

With these and other friendly talks, Francis soon won the complete confidence of the novices. But a year later, when the novitiate was transferred from Arizafa to San Francisco del Monte, a mountainous solitude near the town of Montoro, he found that there was other work to do than that of guiding his little brothers to a more fruitful knowledge and love of God. Even though Montoro was in an isolated valley, word of his preaching abilities already had reached the townsfolk and they had petitioned the superiors that he be allowed to come down into the town from time to time to instruct them in religious matters.

"We need a man like Father Francis," they insisted. "Our children need him, too."

So it was that once or twice a month the Novice Master left his friary home to preach to the people of Montoro. On such occasions the whole town turned out to greet him, the children leading the way up the winding mountain road and singing hymns and litanies which Francis had taught them. In due course the procession would reach the public square, where for an hour or more the Novice

Master would hold his audience spellbound with parables from the Gospel. Or he would relate stories from the lives of the Apostles, those stalwart men who had found in all the trials and hardships of the world only stepping-stones to an intimate union with God.

"Everything that happens in our daily lives can be turned to good," Francis repeated over and over again. And then, as he had done with the novices, he explained the great value of joy. Troubles greeted with a smile, even though it must be a forced one, lose much of their weight. In fact, sometimes they lose all of their weight and show themselves for the true blessings which they are.

Two years passed, and in the friary of San Francisco, high in the mountains above Montoro, Francis' qualities as a spiritual guide became more and more evident. At the Provincial Chapter of 1582, as everyone had expected, he was relieved of his post of Novice Master and made the Father Guardian. What matter that he was but thirty-three years old? Admired and respected by his fellow-religious, he was surely the very one to hold the important position.

Alas! The new honor greatly disturbed Francis' peace of mind. He who always had found a comforting security in obedience no longer had a local superior to obey. More than that. He was responsible for the spiritual and physical well-being of men much older than himself.

"Dear Lord, what am I going to do?" he prayed earnestly. "Surely this is some dreadful mistake!"

But the Father Provincial and his councillors knew that Francis would make an excellent superior. There was no need to choose another for the responsible post.

Realizing that the decision was unanimous, the new Guardian finally ceased his objections. "So be it," he told himself silently. "But I would rather have had the least place in the house than the one that has been given to me."

A few months later, as Francis was making his morning meditation in the friary chapel, he heard the sound of bells from the distant parish church of Montoro. It was not the slow and solemn dirge of the passing bell. Nor was it the joyful peal that marked the celebration of a wedding. No, it was a frenzied clanging in which there was no respite. Francis curbed his curiosity and tried his best to collect his thoughts. The new work as Guardian was such a great responsibility. Although things had gone smoothly enough so far, he needed help and strength to carry on successfully.

"You'll have to continue enlightening me, Lord," he whispered, stretching forth his arms toward the Tabernacle. "There's so much here that I don't know! So many souls to guide, so many tasks to supervise. . ."

Suddenly the peace and quiet of the empty chapel were shattered by still another sound than discordant church bells. "Father Guardian!" cried an anxious voice. *"Father Guardian!"*

Turning, Francis' eyes widened with amazement. Father Bonaventure had burst through the vestry door and now was standing beside him, his face white, his body trembling like a leaf. Before Francis could ask what was the trouble, the other priest had slipped to his knees. His eyes were glistening with fear.

"The plague!" he whispered loudly, teeth chattering. "It's come to Montoro, Father! Oh, what are we going to do?"

CHAPTER 6

FIGHTING THE PLAGUE

FRANCIS WAS NOT long in making a decision. For several months the plague had
been raging throughout Spain. Now it had
come to their own province of Andalusia and
reached the little town of Montoro.

"I must go to the people at once," he declared,
when the two had stepped outside the chapel. "My
son, will you call the community together? There's
no time to lose."

Father Bonaventure nodded, swallowed hard,
then suddenly hurried after Francis, who was disappearing through the vestry door. "Father Guardian,
I. . .I. . .want to go with you!" he cried.

Francis stopped. "But my son. . ."

"Oh, I know what you're thinking—that I'm
afraid. And I am. But you'll need a helper. . .and
with God's grace even I could do something for the
sick and dying. . ."

Off in the distance the bells of Montoro's parish
church continued their desperate clamor, warning
of the disaster which had struck the town. As they

listened to the awesome sound, the two priests looked at each other searchingly—Father Bonaventure still pale and trembling, yet making every effort to control his feelings.

"You'll let me come with you, Father Guardian, even if I am a coward?"

These words, spoken scarcely above a whisper, sent a wave of admiration through Francis. This was no coward, this young friar before him who was so desperately afraid of pain and sickness. All the more because he was afraid and yet would not give in to himself, he was truly heroic.

Francis reached out and took Father Bonaventure's hand. "Very well, you may come," he said. "But hurry and call the community together. And tell Father Anthony to make ready a quantity of food, wine and medicine. There's no telling what the poor sufferers will need."

So it was that within the hour Fathers Francis and Bonaventure set out for Montoro, laden with supplies. And what a tragic sight greeted them as they made their way down the twisting mountain road! Half-crazed with fear, scores of townsfolk were fleeing from the stricken community—on foot, by muleback, in ox-drawn carts and wagons. As the first of these came abreast of the friars, they paused breathlessly.

"Men are dropping like flies back there, Father!" screamed one young woman. "Oh, it's dreadful . . ."

"Yes, you mustn't even try to get into the town!" cried her husband. "The only safe place is up here in the mountains."

Francis looked at the terrified faces about him—the men, women and children whom he had come to know on his preaching trips to Montoro. Poor, poor souls! There was so little now that he could do to save them from the plague. . .

"How many have died?" he asked quickly.

A white-haired man, Montoro's cobbler, shook his head. "There's no telling, Father. But this much is certain: anyone who can walk or crawl is getting out of Montoro. You *must* turn back!"

"But the parish priest—is he all right?"

Again the cobbler shook his head. "I don't know, Father. When we heard that the mayor was dead, and the blacksmith's boy, we didn't ask any questions. We just. . .*came!*"

Suddenly the cobbler's wife uttered a piercing scream. "Look! They're setting fire to the mayor's house!"

At once all eyes turned toward the valley, and amidst the groaning and sobbing about him, Francis felt his heart sink. It was true. Columns of dense smoke were rising from the imposing white structure near the public square. Here and there smaller fires were raging, too—sure signs that the plague had struck in force and that the terrified citizens were doing what they could to stem its progress.

With a hasty blessing for the little group, Francis grasped his bundles in a firmer grip. "We mustn't waste any more time," he declared. "Come, Father Bonaventure. Those people need us."

Within half an hour the two had reached Montoro, and by noon they had given the Last Rites to dozens of souls. Never had Francis witnessed such suffering as that which gripped the stricken town. Everywhere men and women were collapsing, their limbs seized with a strange palsy, their bodies black and bloated.

"This can't keep up!" insisted Father Bonaventure, his fear of pain and suffering now forgotten. "Why, people are dying in every part of the town. And there's no one to carry away the bodies. . ."

Francis had little time to talk. "We'll do what we can," he announced firmly. "Father, round up the strongest men you can find and instruct them to dig as many graves as they can before nightfall. Those who have died must be buried at once. The bodies must not be left to rot in the streets."

Alas for the labors of Father Bonaventure and his assistants! As night crept over Montoro, a night made fearful by the eerie smoke and flame arising from one stricken house after another, there were still not enough graves. From time to time the church bells clanged again, announcing more deaths. Men, women, children—all were falling victim. Even the parish priest had succumbed, and now there were but two men in Montoro capable of administering the Sacraments to the sick and dying.

Towards midnight Father Bonaventure entered the parish church where Francis had gone to take a brief rest. "Father, what are we going to do?" he asked desperately. "There seems to be no earthly hope for these poor people." Yet even as he spoke,

he stopped short in dismay. In the flame-lit darkness without, his eyes had caught sight of a boy
about six, attempting to climb the church steps.
From the pitiful shaking in the small limbs it was
evident that he also had fallen victim to the plague.

"Holy Mother of God!" gasped the friar. "This
child's just a baby! And all alone at this hour. . ."

As he rushed forward to help the little one,
Francis came quickly behind. "My son, I've
reached a decision," he said. "We must move the
sick and dying to some place outside the town. Take
this boy with you, and see if there isn't a large farmhouse that might serve as a hospital."

Father Bonaventure hesitated. The little newcomer, gasping for breath, had just fallen uncon-
scious at his feet. "Father, please give this lad your
blessing before I go!" he begged.

So Francis lifted his hand in blessing, then
turned on his heel. There was no time to lose if
Montoro's sick and dying were to be moved outside
the town. Clearly the task was too much for Father
Bonaventure and himself alone.

"Lord, please be with us!" he prayed. "Tonight
let us find at least a few helpers. . ."

Very soon this prayer was answered. Although
more than one third of Montoro's population had
fled to the mountains, and another third had fallen
victim to the plague, on his travels during the night
Francis had managed to get in touch with most of
the remainder. As he had asked, these came to the
parish church at dawn to assist at his Mass and to
hear what instructions he had to give.

"Actually, there's no need for any of you to stay here," he told the men and women who gathered before him on the church steps after Mass. "You've the right to protect yourselves in time of danger, to flee to the mountains as your friends and neighbors already have done."

"But what would be the use," objected one man wearily, "now that we've already been exposed to the plague?"

His wife nodded. "Yes, and if we did go we might die on the way."

Francis took a deep breath. "Then that means you'll stay and help, good friends?"

For a long moment the husband and wife looked at each other, realizing full well what their decision meant. If they refused, those standing about probably would do the same. Then fresh panic would result. If they agreed, the tension would ease and Father Francis would have plenty of helpers.

"All right, we'll stay, Father," they said finally. "And we'll do what little we can to help."

With a silent prayer of thanksgiving, Francis came down the church steps to grasp the hands of man and wife in true gratitude. Then he turned hopefully to a young girl standing nearby. "And you, Isabel— you've a wonderful way with children. Could you . . . would you . . . look after the little ones?"

Startled at finding Francis singling her out for a special work, young Isabel Fernandez paled, then hid her face in her hands. "Oh, Father! I'm too afraid!" she sobbed. "I couldn't be of use to anyone. . ."

Francis' eyes were full of sympathy. Quickly he looked about for Father Bonaventure, then beckoned to him. "Offer a special prayer that Isabel and the rest of us can say with you," he whispered. "But do it quickly."

So Father Bonaventure advanced to where Francis had been standing. His face was pale and drawn, for in twenty-four hours there had been hardly any time to eat or rest. Yet there was a surprising strength in his voice.

"Heavenly Father, we're surrounded with danger and we don't know what to do," he said, Francis and the others repeating the words after him. "We're afraid of suffering and death. But we know that You love us...and that You've made us to be happy with You forever in Heaven. You'll permit nothing to happen that isn't for our good...and Your glory. Oh, Father, increase our faith and courage! We give ourselves to You as little children...Give Yourself to us as a true Father. Be with us during these dreadful days and nights...and help us to do Your Will. Through Christ Our Lord. Amen."

These simple words had an astonishing effect upon the little group. Throughout his prayer, Father Bonaventure had used the word "we," thus admitting that he also was afraid. And, by repeating Father Bonaventure's words, Francis had acknowledged his fear, too.

"Why, we're not alone after all!" was the thought which filled one mind after another. "In one way, we're no different from these good Fathers..."

So it was that every face brightened just a little when it was announced that, to lessen the danger of contagion, a large farmhouse outside the town was to be made into a hospital. At once several of the women volunteered to go and give it a thorough cleaning. As for the men, some agreed to carry the sick there, others to continue with their labors of digging graves and burning houses which were known to be contaminated. Still others would prepare food and drink for the stricken and for those who were caring for them.

"And you, Isabel?" asked Francis gently. "Do you think you could help a little, too?"

The girl hesitated. Then a strange new courage dawned in her eyes. "I'll do what I can for the children, Father," she said. "Truly I will."

Francis smiled—gratefully, understandingly—then turned to his other friends. "God bless you all," he said. "I've a feeling that everything's going to get better now."

True enough. As the days passed, there were fewer and fewer deaths to report. Then, after a month, none at all. Certainly there was still much sickness in Montoro, but by now the plague seemed to have spent itself. Whether this was because of Francis' precaution of isolating the sick in the hospital outside the town, or by reason of his fervent prayers, no one seemed able to decide. But this much was certain. Until recently everyone had admired the Father Guardian as a fine preacher and teacher. Now all agreed that he was also the greatest and the holiest man whom they had ever known.

"Where would we be but for him?" they asked one another, shuddering. "Why, he saved our lives!"

"Yes, but so did Father Bonaventure," insisted little Martin Aragon, the six-year-old lad whom the younger friar had rescued on the church steps. "Oh, and he knows so many wonderful stories. . ."

Francis encouraged the boy to tell all who would listen of Father Bonaventure's fine qualities, even putting in a word himself from time to time. For instance, surely Rafael Alarcon, Beatrice Melendez and Manuel Luna owed their present good health to the medicine which Father Bonaventure had given them in the early stages of their illness. This mixture of wine and herbs had worked wonders for them, as well as for countless other poor sufferers. And who had discovered the extraordinary remedy? Why, Father Bonaventure, of course! Therefore, who was responsible for the final victory over the plague?

"But *you* prayed, Father!" declared Isabel Fernandez. "And in a really wonderful way! Why, one night in the hospital when the children were sleeping and you thought no one was about. . ."

"Sssh!" interrupted Francis gently. "You were tired that night, Isabel. Perhaps you mistook Father Bonaventure for me."

But the girl shook her head vigorously. "That would have been impossible, Father. There was the brightest light all around you. . .and you were speaking in a clear voice. How could I have been mistaken?"

Poor Father Francis! There seemed to be no way

out of it. The people of Montoro really were convinced that he was the saint and hero, rather than Father Bonaventure.

Then one afternoon events took a sharp turn. A little girl, her eyes wide with fear, arrived at the parish church where once more Francis had established his headquarters. Looking neither to right nor to left, she made her way swiftly up the darkened aisle to where the grey-clad friar was lost in prayer before the Tabernacle. Then suddenly she burst into tears. The message she brought was such a dreadful one!

"Father, you must come at once!" she sobbed, clutching frantically at Francis' sleeve. "Father Bonaventure's caught the plague. . .and there's nothing they can do to save him. Isabel says so. . ."

...SWIFTLY UP THE DARKENED AISLE TO
WHERE THE FRIAR WAS LOST IN PRAYER.

CHAPTER 7

TO AMERICA!

A T ONCE FRANCIS got to his feet to follow the child to the hospital. And what sorrow awaited him there! Worn out from weeks of labor among the plague-stricken, Father Bonaventure had just fallen ill of the dreadful malady himself. Even worse. The medicine which he had given so often and so effectively to others now was proving strangely useless.

"Can't you help him, Father?" cried Isabel anxiously. "You've saved so many by your prayers..."

Francis looked at the young priest, moaning and gasping for breath, the dark shadow of the plague already heavy upon his face, then shook his head slowly. "No," he muttered. "I believe God wants him."

In twenty-four hours Father Bonaventure was dead—a report that saddened every heart in the town. But when Francis made known the young friar's last words, everyone's grief was mixed with holy awe. On his deathbed Father Bonaventure had spoken these extraordinary words:

"Lord, there are so many here who fear to give themselves to You to do Your Will. Won't You let my little sufferings win for them this grace? Please. . ."

"Those were the words of a true saint," declared Francis, joyful tears glistening in his eyes. "Oh, my friends, we must never forget them!"

So it was that Father Bonaventure's grave (dug by Francis' own hands) soon became a place of pilgrimage. Every day men and women went there to pray, not so much *for* the dead friar as *to* him. Well they knew that he had never worked any visible wonders, such as Francis himself had done, yet it was now clear that his life had been wonderfully successful. At the plague's outset he had realized his own human nothingness as never before, his fears of this and that, but nevertheless he had not hesitated to give himself completely to God to do with as He willed. The result? Instantly the disturbing fears had vanished. A host of dangerous and unpleasant duties had been perfectly accomplished, with dozens of lives saved and unnumbered souls made ready for a peaceful entrance into eternity. By his actions Father Bonaventure had proved that the most ordinary people can become holy in a short time if only they will give themselves completely to the Heavenly Father to do with as He wills.

Francis never tired of preaching this doctrine of abandonment to God's Will—the secret of lasting joy in this life—and always used Father Bonaventure as a truly fine example. Later, when he himself

fell ill of the plague and it seemed that he was
about to join Father Bonaventure in Heaven, there
was not the anguish in Montoro which one might
have expected. So Father Guardian had hoped to
be a missionary to Africa, had he? Well, evidently
it was not God's Will. Instead, He had planned that
Francis should spend just thirty-four years on earth,
then go to Heaven to be perfectly happy with Him
for all eternity. Someone else would work for souls
in Africa.

So convinced was Francis that he would never
recover from the plague that his fellow religious
were convinced also, and the townsfolk as well
proceeded to resign themselves to the loss. There
were tears, of course, and regrets, for the youthful
Father Guardian was beloved by all. Then one day
the report from the hospital was unexpectedly
encouraging.

"Father Guardian's getting better! Unless something unforeseen happens, he'll be up and around
in a few weeks!"

What joy in Montoro now! Soon there would be
those wonderfully inspiring sermons in the public
square, the lessons in catechism for the children,
the encouraging visits among the sick and needy.
Oh, in a little while life in Montoro would return
to its normally happy pattern because God had
spared a faithful and loving servant!

But Francis had no desire to return to his former
way of life. Pleading poor health, he petitioned his
Father Provincial for a transfer—adding hopefully
that perhaps later on he could be of some use as

a missionary—in Africa, for instance. As always, many workers were needed there.

The Father Provincial was fully aware of Francis' fine qualities, as also of the real reason for his wanting to leave Montoro: namely, to escape the honors now being heaped upon him for his heroism during the plague. Accordingly, he considered both suggestions carefully. But after days of thought he would agree only to the first. Yes, Francis might leave San Francisco del Monte. A change of residence, to the Friary of Saint Louis in Granada, probably would do him worlds of good. But going to Africa as a missionary was out of the question. Spain needed worthy priests, too.

Francis gave no sign of his keen disappointment. "Thank you, Father," he said quickly. "Granada's a big city. I'll do my best for souls there."

And so it came to pass. During the next five years, Francis endeared himself to hundreds of new friends by his preaching, teaching and works of mercy in the great city of Granada.

Then one day an unexpected thing happened. The Father Provincial informed Francis that he might be a missionary after all, and to a field which he had never considered—the wild forests and jungles of Tucumán, a district in northern Argentina.

"*America!*" breathed Francis, overcome at the mere thought. "Oh, Father! How wonderful!"

The Father Provincial agreed, but he grew serious as he looked at the eager face before him. "Yes, it is wonderful. But remember this, my son: the work there is very difficult and dangerous. You don't have to go to America unless you wish to."

Francis' eyes glowed. "Oh, but I want to go, Father! And with all my heart! When may I leave?" The older religious smiled. "Sit down," he said. "There's quite a bit to explain before I can answer that question."

So Francis sat down, more excited than he had been in many years. He was to be a missionary after all! To save souls for Heaven! To preach and teach among pagan tribes. . .

In just a few minutes the Father Provincial was setting forth a statement of facts and figures. Recently he had received a letter from Philip the Second, King of Spain. In it, His Majesty had asked that a group of friars be sent with certain royal officials to colonize and Christianize various regions in the New World. Peru, conquered for Spain by Don Francisco Pizarro some fifty-odd years before, already had several churches and convents, especially in the cities of Lima and Cuzco. But there were still vast sections in the interior where the people were ignorant of the True Faith. For many years the holy Franciscan Father Balthazar Navarro and his companions had been doing what they could for the poor souls of Tucumán, traveling through forest and jungle, over mountains and into valleys, preaching and baptizing wherever they went. Yet they needed helpers, many helpers. If the Father Provincial could secure some volunteers from among his friars. . .men who were not afraid of hardships or even of real danger. . .

"Naturally I thought of you, Father Francis," said

the latter, smiling just a little. "I suppose you know why?"

Francis also smiled. "Yes, Father. Because for twenty years I've wanted to be a missionary—ever since I joined the Order. But I never dreamed of going to America, you know. Somehow Africa seemed to be the place."

"That's because you're more familiar with Africa. After all, it's nearer home and you've had a few chances to see and talk with those who've been there. But soon you'll have the chance to see and talk with Father Balthazar about the New World. He'll be in Granada one of these days for a little vacation."

Within a month Father Balthazar Navarro arrived at the Friary of Saint Louis—a tall, spare man, his face tanned by years of exposure to the sun and wind.

"Well, where are my helpers?" he asked cheerfully. "I hear that there are four of them."

At once Father Didacus Pineda stepped forward, followed by Fathers Francis Torres, Francis Leiva and Francis Solano. For a moment there was silence as the seasoned missionary surveyed the little group before him with a critical eye. Then he smiled broadly. "I think you'll do," he said. "I think you'll do very well indeed. There's just one thing."

"Yes?" said Father Didacus, a trifle anxiously. "What is it, Father?"

Father Balthazar smiled again. "It's this. You've been told that I'm to have a vacation before returning to America. Well, that's not so, Fathers. There's a boat sailing from Cadiz for Cartagena this week. Passage has been arranged for the five of us. I suggest that you get your things in order and be ready to leave here in two days. You see, there's an enormous amount of work waiting for us in the New World. The sooner we get at it, the better."

Father Balthazar's enthusiasm was so contagious that in a matter of hours his new assistants were regretting that there had to be even a two-day delay. What a wonderful man was Father Balthazar! And what enormous good he must have accomplished during his years of missionary travels! Truly, they were most fortunate to have this courageous and experienced priest as their superior.

On the overland trip from Granada to Cadiz, and later on the long sea voyage via Haiti to Cartagena and Panama, Francis and his companions never tired of listening to Father Balthazar's account of conditions in the New World.

"It's this way," he explained. "Most of the New World belongs to Spain, since Francisco Pizarro and his men overran the west coast and conquered the Indians back in 1532. In the last fifty years, thousands of Spaniards have gone to Lima and other cities with the idea of making fortunes for themselves. And quite a few have succeeded in doing just that."

"I guess Lima's a place of opportunity, all right," said Father Didacus thoughtfully. "A cousin of mine, just a poor man in Seville, went there a few years ago and staked a claim to a gold mine. Now, from all accounts, he's really wealthy. Why, in one

FRANCIS AND HIS COMPANIONS NEVER TIRED OF
LISTENING TO FATHER BALTHAZAR.

of his recent letters he said that he had more than five hundred slaves!"

Father Balthazar nodded. "Yes, and more than one gold mine, too, I'll wager. You see, the Andes abound in gold. Before Pizarro's time, the natives thought nothing of using it for their most ordinary needs—even for cooking utensils, since it was so beautiful. They decorated their houses with it, too. Ah, but it's a different story now. . ."

A shadow crossed Francis' sensitive face. "Tell us again how things are for the natives these days, Father," he said.

So for still another time Father Balthazar launched into a description of what the Spanish invasion had meant to the Indians of the New World. And as he spoke, his voice grew passionate and tense. The men who had come from Spain with and since Pizarro had been Christians—yes. They had brought with them the customs and civilization of Europe, as well as Franciscan and Dominican missionaries to spread the True Faith. But some of them had also brought a greed for gold and for power and a shameful disregard of the rights of others. As a result, the missionaries frequently had found it difficult to prove the worth and value of the Christian Faith. There were so very many of the Spanish settlers who showed in their lives how little they thought of the Ten Commandments.

"Many natives have died because they were forced to work in the gold and silver mines for our countrymen, and under the most wretched conditions," announced Father Balthazar. "Before Pizarro came, the Indians lived peacefully enough—raising crops, contributing toward the maintenance of the Inca or king, weaving excellent cloth from the wool of the alpaca and llama, and making fine pottery. But they worshiped the sun, which they considered to be God."

"And were there no wars, Father? No abuses of any sort?" asked Father Francis Leiva.

The speaker hesitated. "Things were far from being ideal, Father. There were wars, and prisoners were treated very cruelly indeed. By and large, however, life under the Inca (whose name was Atahualpa) went fairly smoothly, as far as material things go. Everyone had enough for his own needs, and it was taken for granted that no one should rise above the station in which he was born. Atahualpa reigned supreme. And since the possession of gold, silver or precious gems was possible for everyone, and the sick and aged were taken care of as a matter of course, there was no thought of piling up a personal fortune. Greed for gold was quite unknown."

Suddenly Father Francis Torres turned toward his superior. "How is it that Pizarro and his few followers conquered the Indians so easily?" he asked. "Surely the Inca had thousands of loyal subjects who were ready to die for him?"

Father Balthazar nodded vigorously. "Yes. But the Spaniards had firearms, remember. The crude weapons of the natives were of little use against these. Besides, there was a civil war going on between Atahualpa and his half-brother Huascar, which meant that the Indians were disorganized and in a poor position to drive out the foreigners. More than that, Atahualpa and his followers were really puzzled by the Spaniards and their strange greed for gold. So, as was their policy whenever they met a people different from themselves, they decided to withdraw into the mountains rather than plot a detailed campaign. They would wait and see if they couldn't outwit these pale-faced newcomers."

"But Pizarro followed the Inca into the mountains, didn't he?"

"He certainly did. And by trickery and superior weapons, he captured Atahualpa, executed him, then proclaimed himself Governor of the whole kingdom."

"And how did the Inca's people take this?"

"Why, they never got over the blow. Without their leader, they were no more than little children and made a poor showing against the Spaniards."

"And now we go to convert the sons and daughters of these poor people," mused Father Didacus softly, "to prove that we have the True Faith, despite the dreadful things that some of our countrymen have done in this New World."

Father Balthazar shook his head. "No, it's not quite that way, Father. Certainly we'll see descendants of the Inca's people on our way to Tucumán— in Trujillo, Lima and other towns. But Tucumán and the neighboring region were never part of the Inca kingdom. In fact, the natives of northern Argentina, where we are headed, are quite different from those in Peru."

"You mean they don't know about Pizarro's coming into Peru and conquering it, Father? They won't distrust us because we're Spaniards?"

Father Balthazar was silent for a moment. Then he gave a deep sigh. "Fortunately the Indians of Tucumán love and trust us who work among them," he said. "As for Pizarro—well, they don't need to know about him in order to be suspicious of white men in general. They've seen plenty of unfortunate examples during the last fifty years."

"But surely not all the Spanish colonists are evil, Father! Aren't there many churches and convents in the New World that they helped to build? And orphanages and hospitals?"

At these words some of the gloom vanished from the eyes of the older friar. "Yes, thank God. There have been many generous souls among the colonists. Would that there were still more of them, though. Then our work with the Indians would be far more fruitful."

As the days passed and the vessel moved steadily through the waters of the Caribbean toward the harbor of Cartagena, Francis found himself pondering certain facts very often.

"Even if all our fellow Spaniards gave good examples in this New World, it would still be hard to convert the natives," he told himself. "After all, for centuries they've practiced all kinds of pagan rites. It wouldn't be easy to show them their error. Then there's the matter of language. . ."

The Indians of the New World had many dialects.

A missionary who hoped to preach and teach effectively must learn these dialects—even as Father Balthazar had done. There was the matter of transportation, too. Roads were few and far between in the country for which they were headed. In fact, Tucumán was some fourteen hundred hazardous miles from Lima, and the only means of travel was on foot or by muleback. Even when one had successfully crossed the snow-covered Andes, there were still the uncharted rivers in the interior, the swamps and jungles infested with wild animals, poisonous reptiles, deadly fevers. . .

Suddenly a little smile lighted Francis' face. The task facing his companions and himself was so gigantic as to make the bravest man among them tremble. But what was the use of worrying?

"Our one hope is to put ourselves completely into God's hands," he thought. "After all, it's His work that we've come to do. He will see that everything turns out well."

CHAPTER 8

MIRACLES AT SEA

IN DUE COURSE the vessel completed its long voyage from Cadiz to Cartagena. A short stop was made there, after which the journey was resumed again, across the Gulf of Darien to Panama. But since there was no waterway through the Isthmus, the passengers found themselves faced with the arduous task of walking across this narrow strip of fever-ridden land which separates the Caribbean Sea from the Pacific Ocean.

It was a painful journey, with many collapsing along the way by reason of the great heat and the lack of pure drinking water. But Francis and his companions persevered, despite the hardships, and on the morning when they glimpsed the Pacific Ocean for the first time they speedily forgot all previous difficulties. A boat was riding at anchor here, ready to take them down the west coast of the continent to Callao, the port of Lima. God willing, in a short time they would be well on their way to Tucumán, that section of northern Argentina where Father Balthazar had labored for so long.

"How wonderful!" Francis thought. "I've waited more than twenty years for this day!"

But very soon all joy faded. As the friars went on board the new vessel, together with a motley group of soldiers, adventurers and officials of the Spanish Crown, a distressing scene met their eyes. Horses, cattle and large quantities of firearms had already been loaded into the hold. Now several hundred Negroes, naked or at best clothed in a few poor rags, were being forced from the dock over a narrow runway leading to a door in the ship's side close to the water's edge. And how they struggled to escape! The air was filled with their screams. And with another sound, too—the cracking of heavy whips as numerous Spanish overseers hastened to and fro, endeavoring to force the poor captives into the ship.

"Slaves," announced Father Balthazar tersely as Francis, horror-stricken, stopped short before the dreadful spectacle. "They've been picked up in Puerto Rico and Haiti and will be sold later on in the market in Lima."

Even as he spoke, the air resounded to the angry oaths of the Spaniards in charge. "Move on there!" they were shouting. "Do you think we can stay here all day?"

Francis shuddered as he saw the slaves, one after another, cringe beneath the lash, then stumble into the hold, their dark faces twisted with terror. But as the minutes passed and the heavy whips continued to descend without mercy upon the victims, he could restrain himself no longer.

"Stop!" he cried out desperately. "These are *people*—not animals!"

Alas! The Spaniards did not even hear his words, for added to the shrieks of the slaves were the bellowing of the frightened cattle, the neighing of the horses, the general coming and going of passengers and crew with their boxes and bundles.

After the boat had set sail, and the cries of the slaves had died away to a hidden murmur from the depths of the hold, the dreadful memory still remained imprinted deeply on Francis' mind. In all his forty years he had never witnessed such cruelty. How could Christians treat fellow human beings so heartlessly? How could they beat them, curse them—*sell* them?

"Dear Lord, let me do something for these poor people!" he thought. "Why, they've been stolen from their homes. . .and probably not one is baptized!"

As the boat pushed southward toward the port of Buenaventura, the Captain assured Francis that there were some four hundred slaves now locked securely beneath the deck, and all of them were pagans.

"Black beasts, that's what they are," he announced cheerfully. "Dirty, stupid black beasts. But they'll bring a good price in Lima."

Francis stared, dumbfounded, wondering whether the Captain had ever learned that all men were created by God to be his brothers in Christ. "Do you suppose I might visit these poor people?" he asked gently. "If they're pagans, it's only because no one has ever told them of our Holy Faith. I'd like to do that, Captain."

The Captain was beside himself with horror at these words. "*You* want to go into the hold, Father? Why, it's nothing but a filthy hole! No light, very little air. Why, those slaves are crawling with filth and vermin!"

"I know. But if they can stand it, then so can I. And my visits would last only an hour or two at a time."

Francis prayed fervently that the Captain would not stand in the way of his plan to teach the slaves in the hold of the ship. Hadn't God called Francis to be a missionary? And here were people desperately in need of hearing about Christ and the True Faith. Four hundred unbaptized souls, locked beneath his feet in a stifling dungeon! Four hundred places in Heaven might be empty for all eternity, because no Christian hand had administered the Sacrament of Baptism!

So it was that Francis began to instruct the slaves in the holy Catholic Faith. He told them about God, about His Son Our Lord Jesus Christ, about how He had died for them, and about how He had taught the one True Religion. He told them of God's love and mercy to those who truly repent of their sins; he told them of Baptism. He told them about Hell—and about Heaven.

It was a wonderful place, he said, where they could be happy with God forever, and where pain and sorrow were unknown. God had made it for those who loved Him. It was a gift, to be accepted or rejected by each living soul upon earth—whether black or white, rich or poor, young or old. It was for slaves, too, and could be *their* inheritance very soon—*if they wished*, if they would make the decision to believe in Our Lord and renounce their sins.

The slaves were listening. Who was this man who cared about them? Who came to them as a friend, as a father, and who told them that the true God wanted them to be His own children! They wondered, and they kept on listening.

Thus the days went by in the Pacific Ocean, that ocean named for its peaceful surface, in contrast to the turbulent Atlantic. But the calm was not to last. As the ship entered the Gulf of Gorgona (about one hundred miles south of the Isthmus of Panama), a dreadful storm arose. For hours the Spanish vessel pushed ahead, buffeted by strong winds and a heavy tide. Then towards midnight there was a sudden and sickening crash. Far off its course, the vessel had foundered upon a reef! A great hole had been torn amidships, and now tons of water were pouring into the hold where the firearms had been stored.

Panic broke out at once. Passengers and crew sprang screaming from their beds, groped in the darkness for what possessions they could find, then ran madly toward the deck. But there was little security there, for mountainous waves were bearing down upon the stricken vessel and the wind was of hurricane strength.

"Dear God, help us!" gasped one man, whom

Francis knew to be a relative of the Viceroy in Lima. "Don't let us die in our sins!"

"Captain! Where's the Captain?" shrieked another. "He can't let us drown like rats!"

Quickly Francis and his priest companions went about among the passengers and crew and gave general absolution. But out on deck amid the drenching waves, the fury of the wind, the screams of the terror-stricken echoing through the darkness, Francis suddenly remembered the four hundred slaves locked in the hold. Unless they were released at once, there would be no chance for them to save their lives. Perhaps even now the water had reached them . . .

"Of course someone must go to those poor people!" declared Father Balthazar when Francis hastened to him. "Get the keys to the hold from the Captain. And take Father Didacus to help you."

So Francis and his companion hurried into the depths of the doomed ship, praying fervently that they would not be too late and that they carried the right keys. Their prayers were answered. In a few moments, the locks and bolts had been released and the terrified slaves in the hold were free to rush into the passageway that led upward toward the deck.

For a moment Francis gazed compassionately upon these unfortunate brethren. How frightened they were! And some seemed even too dazed to understand what was happening.

Francis knew he must work quickly, for death could come at any moment. These souls created by

God for eternal happiness *must* be brought to Him before it was too late! Calling out above the noise, Francis reminded these fellow human beings of the wonderful truths he had been teaching them— about God, Jesus Christ, the True Religion, Baptism, the salvation of their souls. But would they even listen? Or would fear for their lives shut out every other thought? Francis prayed with all his might for these dear souls.

But lo, they were listening! Their hearts were open, they believed, and they were begging for Baptism—the key to Heaven. It was a miracle, a miracle of grace!

Francis lost no time. Moving quickly, he poured the saving waters over one bowed head after another: "I baptize you in the name of the Father, and of the Son, and of the Holy Ghost."

The water became deeper—ankle-deep, knee-deep, in some places even neck-deep. Francis labored on. Each one was another soul for Heaven! "Lord, please give me time!" he silently prayed.

Finally, he was finished. The Holy Ghost was now dwelling in hundreds more souls through Sanctifying Grace.

The ship's boat was able to hold a number of occupants, and it had been launched in a desperate effort to reach shore. But Francis had certainly not been on it. He must stay with his new spiritual children, not to mention the other desperate passengers, now half-paralyzed with fear. . .

The storm raged on. By now the crippled vessel had all but broken in half. Both halves were

HE POURED THE SAVING WATERS
OVER ONE BOWED HEAD AFTER ANOTHER.

doomed, but one half was starting to sink already.

How long would the battered wreckage remain afloat? How long would it be before those on the fast-sinking half of the ship would be swept into the sea? Francis did not know, and he had no time to spend wondering. Calling out above the noise, he would address words of encouragement to the precious souls who could still hear him.

Thus while the wind blew his grey habit this way and that, and the water deepened over the sloping deck where so many were clinging frantically to life, Francis continued to speak of Our Lord, of love of God, of Heaven. And as he looked down into the black faces raised hopefully toward him from out of the ever-deepening water, Francis experienced a tremendous thrill of joy. How good God was! He had given the great grace of Baptism to these poor outcasts. In a little while some of these black children of God, intended for years of back-breaking labor in Peru, would be among the saints of Heaven. Through God's mercy, the Baptism they had just received had cleansed their souls from all sin. Now he must help them all to persevere in Sanctifying Grace—to persevere in faith, hope and charity—and to accept death peacefully, if that was soon to come.

Then, quite suddenly, a giant wave bore down upon the ship, completely severing the two halves. For one dreadful instant the air resounded to terrified screams as those trapped on that half found themselves hurled into the churning sea. The next, there were only the crashing sounds of the waves and the roar of the wind.

Powerless to help, Francis gripped the railing and stared down at the dreadful sight of these dear people struggling for their lives in the grey-green breakers. Then, as one after another disappeared into the depths, he closed his eyes.

"Eternal rest grant unto them, O Lord," he murmured, tears streaming down his face, his hand upraised in blessing, "and let perpetual light shine upon them. May they rest in peace. Amen . . ."

After this horrible shock, the other passengers were frantic. Surely the same death was in store for them shortly? And if not, would the boat ever return for them?

How was it that Father Francis Solano remained so calm? When he was not encouraging them, he was praying, storming Heaven for help for their miserable selves on this sinking half of a ship. In fact, Francis had predicted that on the third day, they would be rescued! It seemed almost too much to believe.

But what was he doing now? Amazed, the men watched as Father Francis Solano began to scourge himself in order to add force to his fervent prayers to the Heavenly Father for relief. It was a pitiful sight. "Stop!" they shouted above the noise of the wind. "Father Francis, stop!"

But a moment later they looked around in surprise. Heaven seemed to have heard, for the storm had died down almost immediately. A blessed calm descended upon the once-churning waters. And as the group was marveling over this, a second remarkable thing occurred: on a last swell of water, there floated toward Francis a crate of altar candles, which had somehow not yet been swept away. Francis reached out and grabbed hold of the crate. Surely this had been sent by Heaven.

Meanwhile, the ship's boat had struggled toward shore. Soon after setting out, its occupants had beheld the ship cleft in two by a great column of water. Then, as they gazed in horror, half the vessel had sunk beneath the waves. Surely the other half would soon follow!

"We'll never see our shipmates again," stated one of the men sorrowfully.

"Not in this life," echoed another.

That first night on shore was a sad one for the little group. But on the second night, they were startled to see what appeared to be a light far out at sea. How could this be? Hadn't both halves of their unfortunate vessel gone down? And yet . . .?

Some of the men would have to go back. And after much rowing, what did they see in the distance but the half-ship still miraculously afloat!

It was now "the third day" of Francis' prediction. Suddenly, one of the men on board the sinking half-ship sighted the boat in the distance.

"They've come back for us!" he yelled at the top of his lungs.

"I see them too!" called out another. The joy on board was indescribable.

When the rescuers had arrived, they soon heard the story of the altar candles—how they had appeared, and how Francis, waiting till nightfall, had lighted them all at once.

"Did you think we'd see your light?" inquired one of the men from the boat.

Francis smiled. "I knew you would," he said simply.

CHAPTER 9

TROUBLE ON SHORE

PRECEDED BY THE others, Francis now did not hesitate to get in line to climb aboard the boat which was to take them all to safety. But just as he was about to step into the vessel, a swell of water pushed it away! Francis would have to swim a short distance to the boat. So, to make swimming easier, he took off his habit, then rolled it up and tied it with the cord he wore around his waist. Then, clad in his under-tunic, he tossed the habit toward the boat. But unfortunately, it missed the boat and sank into the water, disappearing from sight! There was nothing for Francis to do now but jump into the water and swim to the boat. Soon he was safely aboard.

Just a few moments later, he gave a great gasp. As though a signal had been given, the floating hulk where he and his companions had been stranded was splitting into a dozen parts!

"Father, we left it just in time!" cried a young sailor, scarcely more than a boy. "Look! It's sinking for sure!"

Francis nodded. Yes, the boat was going down. In a little while no one would even know where it lay.

"God has been very good to us," he murmured. "Oh, surely we ought to thank Him for our rescue?"

Eagerly the men agreed, and so Francis began to recite the Our Father. All joined in reverently, timing the familiar phrases to the sweep of their oars. Then, the prayer finished, one of the rescuers furtively touched Francis' sleeve.

"Father, before we get to shore. . ."

"Yes? Is anything wrong?"

Not wishing that his words be heard by the others, the man shifted slightly and leaned over toward the friar. "We're having some real trouble on land," he whispered. "Oh, Father, truly I don't know what to do. . ."

Francis listened quietly as the man explained the situation. Among those who had been saved were some soldiers, some officials of the Spanish Crown and a few penniless adventurers who hoped to make fortunes in the New World. These, lacking shelter, had spent their time on the small beach ahead. But now food was running short. Clothes were in rags, affording little protection against the heat of the day or the chill mists of night.

Beyond the sandy beach, where even now the survivors were huddled forlornly, extended countless miles of jungle. What suitable food could be found in such a wilderness, not to mention drinking water? And what about wild animals? The many

unknown dangers that probably awaited the
uninitiated? To make the picture even blacker, sickness had set in.

"Yesterday two of the men went into the jungle,
Father, and ate what they thought were apples.
Today they're suffering horribly and anyone can see
that they've been poisoned. That's made the rest
of us afraid to touch anything, no matter how good
it looks."

Francis peeked ahead at the coastline. "I don't
know anything about this country," he said, "but
surely there must be fruit and berries in the jungle
that are safe to eat. How else would the natives be
able to exist?"

"That's another thing, Father. There don't seem
to be any natives. We haven't seen a living soul
since we landed. And no wonder, if there isn't any
fit food to be had."

When the boat finally reached the shore, Francis
calmly announced that he was going to go look for
his habit. "How ridiculous!" was the thought that
went through not a few heads. The habit had been
lost miles behind them and had probably sunk to
the bottom of the ocean!

But Francis was not dismayed by any jokes or
remarks from his companions. He simply said, "My
Father St. Francis, who granted me this holy habit
when I entered the Order, will have to return it
to me." So off he went to search the shore.

Soon Francis was back—and he was wearing his
habit! True, it was in a little worse shape than
before, but there it was! And the cord was tied

about Francis' waist, just like before. The doubters shook their heads in amazement. There was definitely something extraordinary about this Franciscan priest.

Now Francis lost no time in going about among the survivors. As he had expected, everyone's spirits were at a low ebb. Some of the men, on the verge of despair, were regretting that they had not perished in the storm. Death by drowning was at least fairly quick. It was much to be preferred to starvation or to being poisoned by tropical fruit.

Father Balthazar had a plan, however. "You see," he said to the Captain, "I want to go for help."

The Captain, his face drawn and haggard, stared in amazement. "*Help*, Father? But how? And where?"

Father Balthazar smiled. "If you can spare me the boat and a few of your men," he explained, "we could start at once for Panama to tell what happened. I know that when the Governor hears what I have to say, he'll send another vessel to help us."

For a moment the Captain was silent. There was scarcely one chance in a hundred that a small boat could make the hazardous journey back to the Isthmus. Yet without supplies there was still less chance that those who had been rescued would live for more than a month or two.

"It'll be a risky journey," the Captain said finally, "but the boat and some men to help you will be yours, Father—*if you're sure you want to do this.*"

The missionary laughed at the doubtful tone.

"Don't worry that I'll change my mind," he said. "In one way, it's much easier to be going back to Panama than to be staying here doing nothing. Perhaps before very long you'll agree."

The Captain looked up curiously. "What do you mean, Father?"

"Just this. You're going to have trouble here, Captain. Lots of it."

"Trouble?"

"Yes. The shipwreck has been a great strain for everyone. In a little while the reaction will set in among those who've been saved. Just wait and see."

Father Balthazar's words proved true. Adding to the problems of food, water and shelter, the spirits of the shipwrecked were dangerously low. Hardly anyone believed that Father Balthazar would reach Panama.

Francis, too, was concerned about the prevailing discouragement. "What these men need is work," he thought. "I just wonder..."

Before an hour had passed, spirits were beginning to rise. Father Francis Solano had gone into the jungle and brought back a great quantity of what seemed to be small red plums. These, he assured the onlookers, would be quite all right to eat. The same was true of some strange-looking fish which he had caught in a lagoon farther down the beach.

"But how do you know, Father?" inquired the Captain anxiously. "I didn't think you were familiar with the trees and plants in this part of the country. As for the fish..."

Francis smiled. "I'm not familiar with the trees or plants or fish, Captain. But after I found the plums and caught the fish, I asked the Heavenly Father in the Name of His Son to let these things provide us with a safe and nourishing meal. Of course He heard me."

As they listened to the calm and confident words, Fathers Didacus Pineda and Francis Torres looked significantly at each other, then disappeared together down the beach. Before anyone had noticed their departure, an appetizing aroma was filling the air. The two friars had managed to make a small fire from driftwood, then had cleaned the fish, cut them into pieces and placed them in tempting rows across the hot embers. In a little while there would be the makings of a real meal here for everyone. . .

Of course there was universal rejoicing at the news. Some of the men burst into tears at the sight of the browning morsels. Others had to be restrained from grabbing them and escaping into the jungle. But in a few minutes, thanks to Father Didacus, order was restored. There was one good-sized piece of fish for each man present, he assured his famished audience, plus four plums. Certainly this was not enough to satisfy anyone's hunger completely, but it would help. The main thing to remember was that fighting and trickery would not make for one ounce more of food. What supplies there were must be divided equally—today and every day. Pushing, grabbing, selfishness of any sort, would not be tolerated.

When the little meal was over, Francis seized the opportunity for which he had been waiting. Now that the men had been fed and were in a better frame of mind, it was time to rouse the desire to do something constructive. Some work in common must be undertaken, else very soon their thoughts would turn in upon themselves, and the black mood which had prevailed that morning would return.

"Dear friends, I'd like to build a little shrine in Our Lady's honor," he said. "But I'm not a carpenter. Is there anyone here who knows about building?"

There was a slight pause. Then three men stepped forward. Yes, they knew something about carpentry. They would be glad to help with the project. Of course, without the proper tools, the shrine would have to be just a simple one. There would of course be no fancy carving, no polished columns...

"But I never thought of having anything elaborate," Francis said quickly. "In fact, perhaps 'shrine' is hardly the word to use. You see, Father Didacus managed to save a little statue of Our Lady from the ship. I thought we might make some kind of shelter for it. That's all."

As he had expected, the building of the simple shrine took everyone's thoughts away from his own troubles. Even those who had little interest in religious matters braved the dim green light of the jungle to search for the right type of branches and leaves. Others concentrated on finding flowers and

THE BUILDING OF THE SHRINE TOOK EVERYONE'S
THOUGHTS OFF HIS OWN TROUBLES.

vines, and when two days had passed, a really attractive framework had been erected around Our Lady's statue.

"We'll come here every day to ask our Mother's prayers," Francis decided. "We'll talk to her as little children, and tell her all our troubles. And of course we'll ask her to bring back Father Balthazar very soon."

For a while all went well. Early every morning services were held at the little shrine—hymns, the recitation of the Rosary, a short instruction. Then small groups went forth on the daily hunt for food, along the edges of the jungle or down to the lagoon. Strict orders had been given that no one was to eat or drink anything which had not first been blessed by Father Francis. That dreadful day when two of the survivors had almost died from eating poisonous fruit had not been forgotten.

As time passed, however, the hunting parties became careless. They no longer placed the fruit and berries in their knapsacks, as had been ordered, to carry them untasted to Father Francis. No. First one in the group, then another, would slyly sample the day's assorted find. After all, the walk in the jungle heat back to Father Francis' headquarters was long and exhausting. Besides, wasn't it rather silly for grown men to have to ask permission to eat this or that food? To kneel for a blessing before tasting the least mouthful?

"I'm not going to do it any longer," declared a defiant young soldier one morning. "Why, Father Francis isn't a native of these parts. I know as much about the fruit and berries as he does."

"So do I," boasted a companion. "From now on I'm going to eat and drink what I please."

CHAPTER 10

SOUTHWARD THE COURSE

THAT SAME afternoon a frightened group of men knelt before Francis and spread out the contents of their knapsacks. Tears streaming down their faces, they told of what had happened earlier that day. Back in the jungle a young soldier and his companion had defied Father Francis' authority. They had eaten heartily of fruit such as this, without waiting for the blessing. Now. . .

"What happened?" Francis asked quickly. "Where are these men?"

The leader of the group hesitated. "In. . .in the jungle, Father."

"Not dead?"

"Yes, Father."

A chill clutched Francis' heart. "Tell me all about it," he said quietly. "Tell me everything."

In just a little while the dreadful story was out. The two young men had mocked Father Francis and the rules he had made. They had laughed at the idea of Father Balthazar's ever returning on another ship with food and supplies. After that they had eaten the fruit, urging their companions to do the same. But no one had felt like eating on that particular morning, although there had been other times...

Francis nodded. "Go on," he said.

"There's not much more, Father. Just a few minutes after they ate the fruit, the men were complaining of pains. They fell on the ground in agony and begged us to help them. Oh, it was terrible..."

"Yes, and then their faces turned green, Father. And they clawed the ground like animals. And they began to choke for breath, rolling over and over... and they called upon you to forgive them..."

"And their eyes were bulging out of their sockets, Father..."

Francis listened to the horrible details as though in a dream. The fruit before him, similar to that which the men had eaten, certainly was not poisonous. Then how could it have caused death? Unless, of course, God had certain reasons for acting thus... for making an example of proud and arrogant souls...

"You must take me to where you left the bodies," he said quietly. "Our brothers must be given Christian burial at once. But I think it would be wiser not to mention to the others anything of what has happened—at least, not just now."

Eventually, of course, the story had to be told, and then gloom descended upon the little encampment as never before. What a dreadful place was this deserted coast! Death lurked everywhere, even in innocent-looking fruit and berries! Why, two months had passed now, and not a single living soul had they seen except themselves! Soon it would be Christmas. . .

"It'll be our last one, all right," was the word passed from mouth to mouth. "We could never live a whole year more in this place. . ."

Again Francis did his best to lift the men's spirits. He reminded them of God's goodness, far exceeding that of the holiest man upon earth—of His mercy, which surpassed that of the greatest saint in Heaven. If they continued to have faith, to look upon God as He truly was—a good and merciful Father—all would turn out well. But since the faces gazing up into his own still lacked even the faintest sign of hope, he presently took his violin, which someone had rescued from the sinking ship, and began to play a religious melody.

"Let us praise God in song," he said. "Come, my friends. Give the Heavenly Father your heavy hearts and see what happens."

The singing of the hymns did relieve the gloom within a few minutes. Thus Francis decided to organize frequent singing periods. The hymns, really prayers, could be offered in preparation for the great feast of Christmas. But on Christmas Eve the regular routine was interrupted.

"We're going to sing carols now," Francis announced joyfully. "We must give a fitting welcome to the Divine Infant on this holy night. And after we have welcomed Him properly, I have a surprise announcement to make."

Setting aside their gloom, the group joined with

Francis in holy songs. Then, after the Infant King had been welcomed, Francis made his announcement: "Oh! What good news! Father Balthazar will be with us in three days!"

The announcement had an electrifying effect. But before anyone could ask questions, Father Francis Leiva (Francis' own confessor) intoned the *Te Deum*, and there was nothing to do but to join in the glorious hymn of thanksgiving. When the thrilling strains had died away, however, the questions came thick and fast.

"Oh, Father! How do you know?"

"Did you get a secret message from Panama?"

"Maybe you had a vision, Father?"

"Our Lady spoke to you, didn't she?"

Standing there before the little shrine, Francis let the questions pour over him like a flood. Then, eyes shining, hands clasped, he admitted that Heaven had granted him a glimpse of the future. While he was at prayer, God had let him understand that Father Balthazar was on his way to the deserted strip of seacoast which had been their home for more than two months. And he would be with them within three days.

Three days! It was such a short space of time, and such a long one, too! But whether short or long, within exactly that time Father Balthazar arrived with food and supplies—smiling and cheerful, showing no signs of the difficulties he certainly must have endured on the trips to and from the Isthmus. More than that. The ship upon which he traveled had orders to take the entire group to

Payta, its next port of call. Here all would remain
for a rest. Then another ship would pick them up
for the southward journey to Callao, the port of
Lima.

At Payta, however, Father Balthazar decided that
he and his friars would go the rest of the way to
Lima on foot. It would give the newcomers a
chance to see something of the country, and perhaps they could also do some good as they jour-
neyed through towns and villages.

So it was that in January, 1590, the five grey-
habited religious began their 600-mile trek from
Payta to Lima, staying close to the coastline.

"Do you know why?" Father Balthazar asked.

Francis and his companions shook their heads,
although Father Didacus did have a suggestion.
"Perhaps it's a good way to make sure of not being
lost," he said.

Father Balthazar smiled. "That could be a reason, but it's not the right one, Father. No, we're
going to stay close to the water so that we won't
starve. You see, coastal Peru is almost a desert.
There isn't any jungle now where we can find fruit
and berries, so our food will have to be fish. And
we'll have to be very sparing of drinking water.
There aren't too many villages along the way where
we can add to our supply."

Soon Francis and the others experienced the
truth of their superior's words. As they pushed
steadily southward, it seemed that the world had
turned into a great wilderness. On their right, the
Pacific crashed in endless breakers. On their left,

crescent-shaped sand dunes marched in regular procession as far as the eye could see. There was not a tree, not a flower or a blade of grass, to break the deadly monotony. Certainly without the fish that were to be found in the coves along the way, it would have been impossible to preserve life in this drab brown land.

"But it wasn't always like this," Father Balthazar hastened to explain as they trudged along. "The Incas and those who preceded them were masters at irrigation. In their day much of this coast was a real paradise. They built great reservoirs and aqueducts up in the mountains and saw to it that water came down to the barren lands and made them fertile. But of course when the Spaniards arrived, agriculture was largely forgotten. Only mining mattered, and gradually enormous areas became desert land again—just like this. You'll see what I mean when we reach Trujillo."

In due course the little group arrived at the city founded by Francisco Pizarro in 1535 and named after his own birthplace in Spain. But it was scarcely Trujillo itself, with its colorful Plaza and fine homes, its churches and convents, which Father Balthazar desired to show to his sons. Rather it was a striking sight about four miles distant—the remains of Chan Chan, a city whose origin went back hundreds of years. It covered many square miles and, on the land side, was protected from invasion by two huge parallel walls. Within these walls, facing courts and parade grounds, were palaces, temples, fortresses, storehouses, dwellings, workshops—all built of drab brown sandy clay, with picturesque designs in gay colors carved into the soft substance. Without being told, Francis and his companions easily understood that only in a rainless land such as the Peruvian coast could this earthen city exist for a single season, let alone for centuries.

"Chan Chan was the capital of the Chimu Empire," Father Balthazar explained, as his four companions stared open-mouthed at the imposing sight. "This Empire stretched along the coast, from Guayaquil in the north to Nazca in the south, and covered some 10,000 square miles. The Chimus reigned here peacefully for generations. Then the Incas came into power in the highlands and began to absorb other peoples. In the beginning of the fifteenth century—not quite 200 years ago—they descended upon Chan Chan and conquered it for themselves."

Father Francis Torres looked at the parallel earthen walls, fifty feet in height, stretching back of the city, with their ends secured in the hills. Despite their great age and the battles they must have seen, they seemed to be in good condition.

"You mean, the Incas stormed this place?" he murmured incredulously.

Father Balthazar shook his head. "No, Chan Chan was known to be too well fortified for that, Father. Another method had to be used."

"Some kind of trickery?"

"That's right. The Incas went up into the hills behind the city and won Chan Chan simply by cutting off the water supply. In just a few days the Chimus had to surrender. You see, with the aqueducts in enemy hands and with no hope of rainfall, there was no other course open to them."

"And then the Incas became owners of the city?"

"Yes, until sixty years ago or so, when Pizarro came along to plunder and destroy."

There were many other interesting things which Father Balthazar had to tell his companions as they walked along. For instance, because they were now below the Equator, the seasons were the opposite of what they had been at home in Spain. December, January and February were summer months— June, July and August, winter months. They would be entering Lima at the height of the pleasant summer weather. More than that. As soon as he could arrange it, Father Balthazar would take them to meet one of the city's real saints.

Francis smiled happily at these words. Generally there was so much talk of pagan Indians, of lax Spaniards, that sometimes he all but forgot that in the New World there were truly heroic souls as well —souls who had given themselves to atonement for the sins of mankind by prayer and sacrifice.

"You mean Archbishop Turibius, Father?" he asked quickly. "We'll be able to see *him?*"

"Yes. A meeting should be arranged quite easily. Unless, of course, the good man is away on a missionary trip himself. He travels a great deal up in the mountains, you know."

Alas! Turibius Alphonsus de Mogrovejo, second Archbishop of Lima, was not at home when the five friars reached his city. He had gone to give the Sacrament of Confirmation to the Indians in Huancayo, a lofty mountain village some three hundred miles away.

"That's a long, hard trip," Father Balthazar admitted. "I'm afraid we'll not be able to wait for him to return."

Naturally there was disappointment at these words, for the friars had hoped to receive the good Archbishop's blessing before setting out for their new home in Tucumán. But Huancayo, over 10,000 feet above sea level, could be reached only after much arduous journeying. At least two months would have to elapse before the Archbishop could arrive there, give Confirmation, visit other villages in the vicinity, then return to his episcopal palace.

"And the longest possible time we can stay here in Lima is one week," Father Balthazar said regretfully. "Ah, well—the Archbishop will pray for us all the more when he learns of our disappointment in not seeing him."

Francis used his week to good advantage. As was only natural, he and his companions were staying at the Franciscan friary, not far from the colorful Plaza upon which fronted the Cathedral and the palace of the Archbishop. Each morning after Mass he started out from here on a brief tour of the city. For years he had heard of the extreme wealth and poverty that existed side by side in Lima. Could all these stories be true? he wondered. Was the ruling Spanish class really as heartless as some would make out?

After careful observation, Francis felt that matters had been somewhat exaggerated. True, there were Spaniards who mistreated their Indian and Negro servants, who led vicious lives and thought only of amassing a fortune for themselves and a high place in government circles. There were careless men, too, who rarely thought of God, much less of asking for the grace to serve Him in their daily lives. By and large, however, the great majority of Spaniards in Lima were good Christians, and generous.

"One look at all the churches and monasteries proves that," Francis told himself. "Why, for a city that was founded less than sixty years ago, there's a truly surprising number of them."

Yes, Lima had a full share of churches and monasteries, besides hospitals and houses of refuge. Some of these were even set aside for particular groups of people. Thus, the hospital of Santa Ana, founded by Jerome de Loaysa, first Archbishop of the city, was for Indians. There was a hospital for lepers, too, and homes for aged priests, for sailors, for foundlings. And all of these—churches, monasteries, hospitals, other institutions—had been built through the generous contributions of the Spanish colonists. More than that. The various religious Orders continued to rely upon the alms of the faithful, not only for the care of the destitute but also for their own needs.

Yet one morning as Francis was crossing through the Plaza on his customary daily outing, he chanced upon a scene that did place the ruling

Spanish class in a sad light. A few yards across the Plaza a swaggering figure in scarlet velvet and lace, plumed hat upon his head, a silver sword at his side, had just been stopped by a ragged Negro boy.

"An alms, *señor?*" the child was pleading hopefully, an anxious smile upon his pinched face. "My mother is so sick..."

The man shook off the small restraining hand with a gesture of annoyance. "Why don't you tell the truth, boy?" he snapped. "You haven't got a mother—or a father. You're a no-good street urchin, too lazy to learn a trade. Be off with you!"

But the ragged youngster held his ground. "Please, *señor,* I do have a mother. And she's sick. And unless I can earn a few pennies for food and medicine, I'm afraid she'll die..."

The man laughed harshly. "Then find yourself some honest work. Don't waste your time and mine in idle chatter. *Understand?*"

Dodging the blow aimed at him, the boy turned and ran swiftly across the Plaza, disappearing like some frightened animal among the flowering orange trees on the far side.

Quick tears came into Francis' eyes at the sight. "What a pity!" he thought. "I know the lad wasn't lying..."

On an impulse he approached the well-dressed figure who now was busily brushing the marks of the boy's fingers from his velvet cape.

"Good morning, my friend," he observed evenly. "That little one had an honest face. Wouldn't it have been a good thing to have helped him?"

The man looked up with a frown, not at all pleased that this unkindness had had a witness—and a priestly one at that. "You know Lima's beginning to have too many beggars, Father," he muttered petulantly. "Why, that boy was the third one this morning to ask me for an alms! By all the saints, if a fourth one turns up. . ."

Then, quite without warning, the impetuous words ceased and the angry flush drained from the Spaniard's face to be replaced by a glow of genuine pleasure. Eyes wide with amazement, he clapped a hearty hand upon the friar's arm. "Why, you're Francis!" he cried incredulously. *"Francis Solano!"*

Suddenly it was as though twenty years had slipped away from Francis' shoulders. He was a novice in the friary at Montilla and he was trying to save the vocation of another novice by telling him what it means to be a saint. But not successfully. . .

"John!" he cried, gripping the other's hand warmly. "John, my old friend. . ."

"WHY, YOU'RE FRANCIS!" HE CRIED
INCREDULOUSLY. "FRANCIS SOLANO!"

CHAPTER 11

A NEW HOME IN TALAVERA

IN JUST A FEW minutes John was pouring out his story. Yes, he had done fairly well in the New World. He had a fine home, a wife and children, likewise a half-interest in a silver mine in Potosí. There was a good chance that soon he would own a gold mine, too—near Canta. But of course it was not enough.

"It'll be another ten years before I can say that I'm really successful," he sighed. "You see, there's a lot of competition here in Lima from rogues and cut-throats, Francis. At first I was afraid of them, of their ways and methods, and that kept me back. But now, well...I've learned quite a lot. And I'm still learning."

Francis nodded, his eyes shrewdly observing the other's face. "I can imagine. And you're happy? You're not sorry that you left us?"

John laughed loud and heartily. He had forgotten his displeasure of a few minutes ago when Francis had seen him refuse an alms to the black boy. Now he was quite himself.

"Sorry?" he cried, his eyes on Francis' patched grey habit. "Old friend, can you see me going about in *that*? Or taking orders from a superior who mightn't begin to have my knowledge and abilities? Freedom was always precious to me, you know. I can't imagine not being able to come and go as I please. . .to invest a little money and watch it grow. . ."

"You haven't answered my question. Are you happy here, John? Really happy?"

Suddenly some of the light-heartedness vanished from John's voice. "Of course," he said, a bit stiffly. "Why shouldn't I be? Just wait until you see my house, Francis—my wife and three boys." Then, hesitating a little: "You can come to see us, can't you?"

Francis smiled. "I think so."

There was but one visit with John and his family, however, for the day of departure for Tucumán loomed large. The town was some 1,400 miles southeast of Lima, and there was much to do to prepare for the journey there. Yet even one visit with his old friend was sufficient to make Francis feel ill at ease. Poor John! Although he possessed a luxurious home, servants, a good wife and family, it was still clear that he was not at peace. In the temporal sphere he was wearing himself out with worry—about how to make more money, about how to keep what he already had from the clutches of unscrupulous neighbors. In the spiritual sphere— well, long ago he had lost interest in that.

"But why?" Francis wondered. "Once upon a

time John was a good lad. He even wanted to be a missionary to Africa. Then suddenly. . ."

It did not take much figuring to arrive at an answer. Twenty years ago pride had disrupted John's life. As a young man in Spain he had chosen to follow his own will instead of that of the Heavenly Father. That was why he had left the Franciscan Order to seek his fortune in the New World. Then, little by little, the pride had grown. John had ceased to pray, to receive the Sacraments, even to think about God in Heaven. Therefore, what was more natural than that now he should never think about Him on earth—never see Him in a Negro, an Indian, a little beggar boy?

"A man's life has absolutely no point when he doesn't think about God either in Heaven or on earth," Francis told himself. "Dear Blessed Mother, can't you help John to realize this? That pride is taking away all his peace and joy? Oh, he'll never have any real happiness until he gets rid of the last little bit of it!"

As he was accustomed to do when asking for a very special favor, Francis enlisted the help of two favorite heavenly friends—Francis of Assisi and Peter of Alcantara. "Pray for John, Blessed Fathers," he begged, "that he may be made worthy of the promises of Christ." But he smiled a little as he recalled those youthful years when he had prayed that some day John would go to God wearing the habit of the Franciscan Order.

"That isn't necessary now," he told himself. "John can give himself to God, and so become a saint, just as he is. Oh, dearest Mother, Blessed Fathers Francis and Peter, obtain what I ask for my old friend! *Please. . ."*

In the weeks that followed, this and other prayers for John were frequently on Francis' lips. But there were also a good many prayers offered for himself and his companions, since by now they were on the road again. And such a road! South from Lima along the barren coast to Arica, thence slowly and painfully eastward into the Andes, over rivers, ravines, along the edges of glaciers, with entire days passing when they saw no living creatures save flocks of llamas and alpacas moving majestically across the deserted slopes.

"Don't be discouraged," Father Balthazar told his companions one day when the going had been particularly difficult. "The air has little oxygen in it up here in the highlands. That's one reason we get so tired. But after next week we'll be going downgrade and breathing will be much easier. You'll see."

Then to take each man's thoughts away from present difficulties, the kindly missionary began to discuss the future. "There are four fairly important towns in northern Argentina," he explained. "First, of course, is Tucumán—from which our entire missionary district takes its name. But we have other missions here, too—Talavera, Santiago del Estero and New Córdoba. Talavera will be our first stop. And here, I might as well tell you, our little party will break up."

Francis was surprised and not a little concerned

to learn that he was to be left behind in Talavera. At first he would stay at the small friary in the town, but when he had learned something of Tonocotes, the local dialect, he would divide his time between Magdalena and Socotonio, settlements of Christian Indians on either side of the Juramento River.

"Don't worry," said Father Balthazar, noting the rather strained expression which suddenly had come over Francis' face. "You've several friends in Talavera who'll look out for you."

"Friends? But how can that be? I've never even been. . ."

"I know. But long ago I sent word to our friars there that you were coming. And to the Governor of the town as well—Don Andres Garcia de Valdes. I know that these good people will help you to get settled."

Francis hesitated. "And you, Father—shall I see you again?"

Father Balthazar laughed heartily. "Of course. I'll be back in Talavera in a few months—just as soon as Father Didacus and the others are settled in their own fields."

It was June, 1590, when Francis took up residence in Talavera. Father John de Castilla, a Spaniard about his own age, gave him a warm welcome and lost no time in taking him about the town and explaining what would be his work.

"The Indians in these parts embrace Christianity very readily," he announced. "You'll be very happy with them. Why, there are no more peaceful reductions in this whole region than the ones at

Magdalena and Socotonio."

"*Reductions,* Father?"

"Ah, that's a new word for you, isn't it?"

"Well, I did hear something..."

"Reduction is another name for settlement, Father. It comes from the Latin word *reducere*—to lead back or to draw together. You see, we've been trying to draw together into Christian communities the Indians of these parts who until recent years led wandering pagan lives."

"Oh, so only Christian Indians live in the Reductions?"

"That's right. In this way they're protected from mistreatment by unscrupulous Spaniards, and also from the bad example of their pagan brothers."

Within just a few days Francis had gained a good understanding of the Reductions and of their value—both in the temporal and spiritual spheres. Remote from cities and towns, they were places where the Indians learned about God and His Commandments first, then about how to make a decent living, either from the soil or from the mastery of some trade. Since evil influences from the outside were quite lacking, life was virtuous, pleasant and productive in the Reductions. If troubles did arise, they were promptly settled by the missionary in charge.

"It's a wonderful plan," Francis declared one day as he walked with the Governor of Talavera, Don Andres Garcia de Valdes, down the main avenue of the town. "Why, this morning out at Magdalena I had at least 25 little boys and girls following me about, begging for stories about God and His saints! Surely a few years back. . ."

"A few years back no Indian in these parts had ever heard of our Holy Faith," said Don Andres emphatically. "We can thank Father Balthazar and those good Franciscans who preceded him for the progress that's been made since. But there's something else that's wonderful, too, Father. Can't you guess what it is?"

Francis' eyes brightened. "Oh, yes—the country about here! It's wild and dangerous, of course, but how beautiful! Such forests! Such fertile valleys. . ."

"No, I don't mean the countryside, Father. It's something quite different. Haven't you noticed it on your trips to Magdalena and Socotonio?"

Francis hesitated. "Perhaps you mean the wild birds—those enormous red parrots with the blue and green tails. . ."

"No, Father. I don't mean the parrots. I mean *you*, the way you've learned Tonocotes. Don't you know that after only fifteen days of study you speak it like a native?"

Francis tried to dismiss the matter with a laugh. "With you for a teacher, Don Andres, why shouldn't I do well?"

Don Andres was in no mood for joking, however. "Father, I know missionaries who spent years. . . yes, years. . .trying to master Tonocotes, and without success. Businessmen, too, who had hopes of finding gold in these parts. But you—well, I don't understand how you've done it, but this very minute you speak Tonocotes better than I do."

Fearful that his rapid mastery of the local dialect might be attributed to his own powers, Francis decided to share a secret with the Governor of Talavera.

"When I came to you for lessons in Tonocotes, I had already asked Saint Bonaventure to help me," he said simply.

"*Saint Bonaventure?*"

"Yes. He's one of the saints of our Order, you know—a very learned and holy man who went to Heaven in the thirteenth century. In fact, he is to us Franciscans what his friend Saint Thomas Aquinas is to the Dominicans—the patron of students."

Don Andres' eyes were wide with amazement. "And you really believe he helped you?"

"Of course. Didn't I pray to him?"

"But that's no guarantee, Father! Why, I've often prayed to the saints for this and that favor, yet very seldom with any success."

Francis smiled. "Every time you pray to the saints to intercede for you with God, Don Andres, they do so. Never fear."

But Don Andres was not convinced. A year ago he had prayed to Saint Joseph that a business investment in Lima would bring a good profit. Well, what had happened? Why, overnight the investment had proved worthless! Even more. For years he had been asking the Blessed Mother that his invalid sister in Spain might improve in health. But had this prayer been answered? No, indeed. According to a letter he had just received, his sister was suffering more than usual.

Very simply, as though to a child, Francis began to talk about prayer. Don Andres must not think that because Saint Joseph and the Blessed Mother had not granted the particular favors he had had in mind, they had not heard his prayers. Far from it. Undoubtedly they had secured for him many better blessings instead. Not until the next life would he realize just how numerous and wonderful they were.

"But I want the blessings I ask for, not any others, no matter how wonderful," objected Don Andres. "Oh, Father! If you knew what hopes I had for that investment. . .and how my poor sister has suffered all these years. . ."

For a moment Francis was silent, visibly affected by the sorrow in his friend's voice. Then suddenly his face brightened. "I know what you must do to have true peace," he said. "Listen. . ."

Francis' plan was a simple one. Each day Don Andres was to continue asking the Blessed Virgin and Saint Joseph to obtain this or that favor. Then, his petitions made, he was to present the most important request of all—namely, that there might grow within him a real knowledge and love of the Heavenly Father and His Will.

"Here's a grace you're sure to receive if you ask for it humbly," Francis declared. "And just think! It has the power to make you into a totally different person—one without fears or worries or regrets. For once you love the Will of the Heavenly Father, you'll experience a really wonderful joy that nothing can take from you. Do you know why?"

Don Andres shook his head dolefully. "No, Father."

"Because then you'll understand that everything which He permits to happen to you is for your glory—and His."

The Spanish official was stirred in spite of himself by the fervor in Francis' voice. "Even the bad investment and my sister's suffering?"

"Yes."

"But I can hardly believe *that!*"

"Of course not. Right now you've only a very weak love for the Heavenly Father. Actually, you're not much interested in His Will. But once you've asked for the grace I just mentioned—oh, how different it's going to be! You'll be one of the happiest people in Talavera, Don Andres—no matter what happens to you!"

The Governor was not too hopeful, but he had faith in Francis and promised to pray as he wished. Every day, in the Name of Jesus Christ, he would beg to grow in a knowledge and love of the Heavenly Father and His Will.

As time passed, Francis helped other people to pray fruitfully, too. Every day he visited the Indians of Socotonio and Magdalena, instructing them in religious matters. And what joy when he brought his violin with him! Never had anyone seen such a wonderful instrument. Under Francis' skillful fingers it could sing with joy or cry out in sorrow almost as though it were human. Dark-skinned

A SONG WITH GOD'S LOVE
FOR MANKIND AS A THEME.

natives came from miles around to hear the wonder, and not a child but ceased its wailing when the grey-habited friar played his selections—hymns which already were familiar to everyone in the Reductions, or Spanish tunes with gay, unexpected rhythms.

Francis had always loved music. As a boy he had passed many a pleasant hour with his violin in the family garden. Later, as a priest at Our Lady of Loreto, in Montilla, Arizafa, San Francisco del Monte and finally in the Friary of Saint Louis in Granada, he had carried on with his music. But surely all these years when he had studied, taught, played and sung for his companions were but a rehearsal for the present performance? The song he was singing now—a song with God's love for mankind as a theme—was meant for a far greater audience than any he had ever known in Spain. It was meant for those dwelling in the New World, in the uncharted regions of Peru and Argentina. Yes, and perhaps still farther away—across the mighty Paraná and Paraguay rivers. Even along the Rio de la Plata . . .

Often a very humble Francis would consider these things, especially that his work as a missionary might be likened to a song, a song for Christ, a song in the south which was only just beginning . . .

"Oh, dear Lord, let me sing it well!" he would murmur. *"Please!"*

Then one day his customary joy was seriously disturbed. Father John de Castilla (who had made him welcome upon his arrival in Talavera) announced that the majority of Indians from the Socotonio Reduction wished to move away.

"They've been threatening to do it for a long time, but now they're really in earnest," he said. "Oh, Father! When these poor souls leave our protection they're almost sure to be enslaved by some unscrupulous Spaniard...or to meet up with pagan Indians and so lose their faith..."

Francis could hardly believe his ears. The Indians of Socotonio wished to leave the friars' care? But surely there must be some mistake! Ever since his arrival among them he had been struck by the happiness on their faces, the interest with which they plied their various skills, above all by the general eagerness to know more about the Religion brought by the Spanish priests who were so kind to them.

"What is it?" he asked quickly. "Why do they want to go?"

Father John's reply was brief and to the point. "They say that their water supply is no good. And they're right, Father. The well at Socotonio dries up at least three times a year. In the past we've been able to manage by bringing over water from Magdalena..."

Francis breathed a sigh of relief. "A lack of water!" he exclaimed, smiling. "Father John, for a moment you had me worried. I thought the Indians had some serious reason for wanting to leave us."

"But a lack of good drinking water is a serious reason! Why, last summer..."

Francis did not seem to hear. "Father, I wonder

CHAPTER 12

THE CRUEL MOUNTAIN TRIBES

SOON AN AMAZING piece of news was making the rounds. A spring of fresh water had been discovered in the very midst of the Socotonio Reduction, and by none other than a comparative newcomer to the neighborhood—Father Francis Solano! Now it would not be necessary for anyone to move away.

"It's a miracle, that's what it is," Father John de Castilla confided to Don Andres in a trembling voice. "Why, if I hadn't seen it with my own eyes...and if there weren't a score of others to back up what I say..."

"Tell me about it," urged the Governor, who had made a hurried trip from Talavera as soon as news of the wonder had reached him. "I can hardly believe that Socotonio has a good water supply at last."

So Father John began to describe the recent marvel. He had accompanied Father Francis to Socotonio, found him a stick...

"A *stick?*"

"Yes, the dead branch of a fig tree. Then we walked about the Reduction with a number of Indians following us. I could see that Father Francis' thoughts were far away. From time to time he would draw patterns on the ground with his stick, look at them intently, then move on."

"How long did you walk about like this?"

"About fifteen minutes. Then suddenly Father Francis' face began to shine like the sun. 'There's good water over there!' he cried, pointing with his stick. 'Come along, my children, and see how well God has provided for us!' "

Don Andres listened carefully as Father John described how Francis had pointed to a certain spot with his stick, then knelt down beside it and begun to dig with his hands. In a minute or two a trickle of water had appeared, growing into a fine bubbling spring in the course of half an hour. And all this in a dry, dusty region where water had never been known to flow before!

"Naturally the Indians are beside themselves with joy," concluded Father John. "Of course they've loved Father Francis ever since the day he first came to work among them. But now—well, they're convinced that he's a saint. They'd kiss the ground he walks on if he'd permit it."

Three years passed, and "Father Francis' Spring" did not fail but grew even more abundant. In fact, the stream that flowed from it was sufficient to turn the wheels of two mills—which meant that now wheat and other grains could be ground quickly and easily instead of by the slow and laborious hand

ALL THIS IN A REGION WHERE WATER
HAD NEVER BEEN KNOWN TO FLOW BEFORE!

method which had been used in the past. Nor did Francis cease his good works for those in the neighborhood. Was there a little child in Socotonio or Magdalena who had difficulty in learning the Catechism? Francis would take him aside and explain everything simply and clearly. Were there sick or aged Indians living at a distance from the reductions who needed the services of a priest? Francis would go to them, no matter what the hour of day or night. Were certain crops not thriving as they should? Francis would bless them, and all would be well.

But not only Socotonio and Magdalena witnessed Francis' zeal for souls. In the course of time, with the friary in Talavera as his headquarters, he succeeded in founding some fifty other reductions. Over and over again, having established his settlements and placed them in the care of one or more friars from Talavera, he would strike out into the wilderness in search of still more pagan tribes. The Lules Indians, between Talavera and the city of Tucumán to the south, were converted to the True Faith by the grey-clad Spanish friar. The Indians of the Gran Chaco, that wild and perilous country in northern Argentina which lies to the east of Talavera, also heard the Gospel from Francis' lips. In fact, he was able to establish permanent missions among the Mataras Indians in that section of the Gran Chaco which lies to the east of Santiago del Estero—a truly remarkable feat, since the tribes there were extraordinarily wild and much averse to settling down in reductions.

As the months passed, Francis became known by an impressive title—"The Apostle of Tucumán." This was given to him not only for the work he accomplished on his various trips to the city, but because he had made all of northern Argentina his mission field and this district bore the same name as the city itself. Truly, the Franciscan Order had never had such a successful missionary in the New World as Father Francis Solano—now forty-five years old. Inflamed with love of God and souls to an intense degree (and so a man of constant prayer and penance), he was also an excellent preacher, with a gift for making himself understood in all the native dialects. He was an accomplished musician, too. Many a time in the depths of the jungle— according to word that drifted back to his head-quarters at the friary in Talavera—he was able to gather together a crowd of Indians merely by play-ing a few notes on his violin. Then, as these chil-dren of the wilderness stared suspiciously, he would break into a gay Spanish air and begin to sing and dance. Before long, his music and his friendliness would have won all hearts. Then, quite simply, he would tell his new friends about the True God. Before an hour had passed, the chiefs would be begging for Baptism—for themselves and for their people. And noting that the newcomer had a won-derful power to cure the sick merely by raising his hand over them, they would be bringing him all their invalids.

"Certainly our good Father is a saint," the friars at Talavera told one another earnestly. "What would our missions do without him?"

Word of Francis' good work also reached Lima, 1,400 miles away, and in 1595, when he had been a missionary for five years, he received an important message from his superiors there. A recent Provincial Chapter had appointed him Custos, or superior, of all the Tucumán missions!

"But it can't be!" he cried unbelievingly. "Why, I don't begin to know enough about missionary life to tell others what to do!"

Yet there was no use in worrying. It had taken a long time for the message of his appointment as Custos to arrive from Lima. It would take just as long for a letter to go back there asking for advice.

Realizing this, Francis reluctantly began to make plans. "I guess it would be well to visit the different missions," he told himself. "After all, that's what a Custos is for. And by talking to other missionaries and seeing what they've done, I ought to learn a great many things that will help me to be a good superior."

So once more the travels began—across northern Argentina to the Paraná River—preaching, teaching and converting with wonderful success. Indeed, during the next six years Francis' name became even more familiar, to Indians and Spaniards alike. Willingly would the various pagan tribes have kept him with them, the Spanish colonists of Tucumán, Santiago del Estero, Corrientes, Santa Fé and Córdoba, but always Francis declined to remain in one place for more than a few months. He was a missionary, he said, whose work it was to sow the seeds of God's Truth in human hearts, tend them for as long as necessary, then give the harvest into the hands of others.

Finally came the day when the now-seasoned missionary arrived at Rioja, a mining town in the foothills of the Andes. "There's a reduction here," he told himself, "but there are many pagan Indians in the neighborhood, too. I wonder, if I went about among them. . .and if I explained things to the Spanish settlers. . ."

As Francis had hoped, the townsfolk of Rioja gave him a warm welcome. They had heard of his wonderful ability to get along with the Indians and were only too glad when he outlined his plan to form a new reduction outside their town.

"By all means go ahead with the idea, Father," said the mayor. "You see, none of us feels easy about the pagan Indians. We know they hate us Spaniards. If you can gather all of them in one spot and see that they don't stir up any trouble, it'll be a wonderful relief. Why, the way things are right now, we can't sleep peacefully in our beds at night for fear of an uprising that will turn into a massacre."

Francis agreed that it was a sad state of affairs all around. The Indians feared the Spaniards, since so many of them in other parts had enslaved and mistreated the Indians. And the Spaniards feared the Indians, since they had heard so many dreadful tales of torture inflicted upon white men in the past. (The stories of cannibalism were sufficient to make anyone's blood run cold!) But, Francis told himself, surely things would be quite different once he had gone among the Indians with the message of the True Faith. . .once he had won their confidence. . .

"I mustn't lose any time," he declared to the people of Rioja who were clustering anxiously about him. "Do you know the name of the Indian leader in these parts?"

The mayor volunteered the information. The Indian leader was an elderly warrior named Peter Cotero. He and his people were encamped a few miles from the town. But surely Father Francis would never be so foolish as to go to see him alone! A special guard of Rioja's bravest men would be assembled at once, fully armed with muskets and swords, and mounted on the swiftest horses. . .

Francis smiled and shook his head. "No," he said gently, "I'll not need a guard. As for weapons— well, I've always found that a crucifix has more power to change men's hearts than a musket or a sword. However, I might take one thing with me. . ."

"A spear?" inquired the mayor hopefully. "We have some good ones with poisoned tips." But even as he spoke his face clouded. "I'm afraid the Indians would never give you a chance to use it, Father."

Francis smiled again. "I wasn't thinking of taking a spear. I was thinking of taking a violin."

The mayor stared. "A *violin?* But what good would that be?"

"Ask me that question in a month's time and I

may have an answer for you," said Francis, "a really interesting answer."

True enough. In a month's time Francis was able to report that Peter Cotero and his entire tribe were ready to embrace the Catholic Faith; and that he had first gained their confidence by going among them as a wandering musician!

"The Indians are something like little children, you know," he said. "They love to sing and dance. So I played for them on the violin and let their chief try his hand at it, too. Before long we were very good friends."

"But their language, Father! It's quite a bit different from Tonocotes. How did you manage to make yourself understood?"

Francis hesitated. Should he tell the people of Rioja that long ago God in His infinite Mercy had given him the gift of understanding, and of being understood in, all the Indian dialects? That his learned and heavenly friend Saint Bonaventure was always near to help him with his missionary work? Then finally he decided against it.

"It seems that Peter Cotero is a very clever man," he said lightly. "He understood me without the least trouble. And his followers seem to be clever, too, for they also followed what I was saying whenever we talked together."

The townsfolk of Rioja had to be content with this explanation, although from the start they noted its weak points and guessed the truth. For instance, it was all very well to say that Peter Cotero and his people understood Father Francis' attempts to speak their language because they possessed a high degree of intelligence. But then how did Father Francis understand *them*—unless he was equally intelligent? *Or unless there was something supernatural about the whole affair.*

"That's it," the mayor announced. "This good priest is a saint and has the gift of tongues—just like the Apostles. Unless I'm much mistaken there'll be some unusual things happening around here."

The mayor was right. Within six months the people of Rioja were enjoying a new and wonderful security. Gratefully they realized the reason for this: that now the pagan Indians of the locality would never rise up to massacre and destroy because under Francis' leadership they had settled down into a model Christian community just outside the town. Here they were learning many useful things, including how to till the soil better and how to produce good crops. Even more wonderful. By now all of them had been baptized, and there was not one who was not eager to learn everything possible about the religion which Father Francis preached.

Yes, all was peaceful within Rioja's new reduction, and it was with happy hearts that the recent converts presently prepared to celebrate the great feast of Easter. Each evening during Holy Week they came together to listen to Francis' explanation of the Passion and Death of Christ. Then, before Mass in the morning, there was a simple description of the ceremonies that were about to follow.

But at dawn on Holy Thursday, just as Francis

was preparing to give his customary little talk,
panic seized the entire congregation. Off in the distance, faint but unmistakable, was the ominous beat
of war drums!

At once Peter Cotero sprang to his feet, knowing
full well what had happened. Pagan Indians from
the mountainous regions west of Rioja had come
down to attack the Reduction. They had heard
numerous tales of the good life there, and of how
Indians and Spaniards now lived on friendly terms
with one another. Enraged by what they considered
to be treachery, they were out to seek revenge on
both groups. Even now they were beginning their
frenzied war dances.

The elderly warrior looked about fearfully. He
and his people had come to church that morning
to pray and to listen to Father Francis, not to do
battle. There was not one man among them who
was armed. But since the enemy was still some distance away. . .

"Kneel down, Peter," said a calm voice suddenly.
"Don't even think of going for weapons."

Peter turned. Father Francis had appeared from
nowhere and was standing at his side. "But you
don't understand!" cried the old chief desperately.
"Those. . .those others are coming *here,* Father!
They know we're Christians now and they want to
offer us in special sacrifice to their gods!"

An old woman fell on her knees at Francis' feet.
"Yes, and they'll torture us first!" she sobbed.
"They'll put out our eyes and then burn us to
death!"

"They'll cut off our fingers, too!" wailed another, clutching frantically at the missionary's grey habit. "Oh, Father! Can't we get away while there's still time?"

Francis looked at the agonized faces before him—the men, grim and silent, who would dash for weapons in a minute if he would but grant his permission—the women, tears streaming down their cheeks, their terrified children clutched fiercely to their breasts. It was a heartrending scene, made even more fearful by the insistent beating of the drums in the hills above the town. But in half an hour, an hour at the most, it would be far worse. Then the enemy would have arrived— hundreds of them, perhaps thousands—armed to the teeth with knives, with poisoned spears and arrows! And not only would they massacre those living in the Reduction. They would go on to Rioja itself, where even now the Spanish residents must be half out of their wits with terror.

For an instant Francis closed his eyes, apparently heedless of the impending danger. But the next minute his voice was ringing out in firm, clear tones. No one was to be afraid. No one was to leave for weapons. No one was to do anything but recite the Our Father—slowly, carefully, *with confidence in God.*

"As for me, I'll take a large crucifix and go to meet our brothers," he said. "God willing, they'll be glad to listen to some news I have for them."

Peter Cotero and his followers could hardly believe their ears. Father Francis called the bloodthirsty tribes *brothers?* And he was going out alone to meet them? Why, they would take him captive at once! As for any news...

"Begin to say the Our Father," ordered Francis again. "And don't stop praying until I give the word. Above all, remember that you're God's children now. As long as you love Him and want to serve Him, nothing can really hurt you."

So it was that the Indians of Rioja began to pray as Francis had bidden, bowing their heads to receive his blessing as he passed among them. But he had been gone only a few minutes when fresh panic broke out. By now the beat of the war drums had become so much faster—and clearer! And the air was filling with bloodcurdling screams as the pagan tribes plunged through the hills in the direction of Rioja. In just a little while...

"We must keep on praying!" cried Peter Cotero, torn between the duty of obeying Father Francis and the natural desire to pit his strength and skill against the approaching enemy. "*We must!*"

With groans and sighs the terrified Indians resumed their prayers as best they could. Where was Father Francis now? Had the enemy seized him? Were they torturing him?

"*...hallowed be Thy Name, Thy Kingdom come, Thy Will be done on earth as it is in Heaven...*"

Perhaps he was being tied to a stake! Perhaps a fire was being built...perhaps sharp knives were being made still sharper...

"*...forgive us our trespasses as we forgive those who trespass against us...*"

Suddenly new terror filled every heart. Without warning the beating of the war drums had ceased, as had the bloodcurdling screams from the hills above the town. Now all was peace. "But what does this mean?" Peter Cotero and his followers asked themselves fearfully, almost forgetting to continue with their prayers. What dreadful things were the cruel mountain tribes plotting? *Above all, what had they done to Father Francis?*

CHAPTER 13

THE WONDER-WORKER

WITHIN AN HOUR these questions were answered, and more happily than anyone had dared to hope. For the silencing of the war drums had not meant that the bloodthirsty mountain tribes were plotting fresh tortures for the citizens of Rioja. No, indeed. It had meant just the opposite.

"I don't understand," Peter told his wife that night. "They say that Father Francis met those furious warriors on the road and made them sit down and listen to one of his sermons. Can you imagine that? Especially when they were on their way here to kill us?"

Peter's wife was also finding it hard to realize the amazing event. "There were twenty thousand of them!" she exclaimed incredulously. "And now nine thousand of them have been converted—and were baptized this very day! Why, they're even planning to stay here and celebrate Easter with us. . ."

Before many weeks had passed the whole story was being told again and again in town and reduction. At Rioja, early on Holy Thursday morning, and by a single sermon, Father Francis Solano had converted some nine thousand Indians—many chieftains and their respective followings of warriors! This fact in itself was astounding, of course, especially since these Indians had been bent on murder, destruction and plunder within Rioja when Father Francis had come upon them. But even more astounding was the fact that he had preached to them in one language and been understood by all, though they spoke various languages and knew only their own language. That is, all heard him speak in their own language, though he spoke only one.

"It sounds just like one of those thrilling stories from the *Acts of the Apostles*," declared a Spanish trader from Córdoba when the wonder was related to him. "But I'm not too surprised. I heard Father Francis preach once, and there's no doubt about it. He has a really marvelous way with souls."

"I'm not surprised either," replied his companion. "I was in Talavera not so long ago and I heard all about the wonders the good man worked for the people when he lived there. In fact, Don Andres the Governor told a fine tale. . ."

"Not the one about the bull?"

"Why, yes. Father Francis and he were going down the street, the Governor on his horse, Father Francis on foot. . ."

"This is one of my favorite stories!"

"Suddenly a wild bull came charging through the streets. Of course everyone was terrified and ran for shelter. Even the Governor forgot everything but his own safety and spurred his horse to a gallop. Then, a few moments later. . ."

"A few moments later he was shaking like a leaf. What a dreadful thing he had done in leaving Father Francis to face the angry bull alone! He was almost too afraid to go back to see what had happened."

"But he did go back."

"Of course he did. And everything was fine. It seems that the bull had decided to charge Father Francis—but the good priest quickly removed the cord from his waist and held it up in front of the bull."

"His *cord?*"

"Yes."

"And the bull stopped?"

"That's right. And to show everyone that the animal was now quite harmless, Father Francis tied the cord around the bull's neck and led him through the streets to the barn where he belonged."

There were many other stories concerning Father Francis which the two friends presently related to each other. In fact, it seemed that there was no end to the wonders which God had permitted the good friar to perform. In the vicinity of Santiago del Estero, for instance, he had established peace between a number of tribes who had been feuding with one another for years. Now these tribes had settled down into a model Christian community. He had done wonderful things in the

FATHER FRANCIS WAS LEADING THE
BULL THROUGH THE STREETS.

cities, too, especially in Córdoba, by making the Spaniards there realize that their sinful lives were bringing them closer and closer to Hell, besides giving scandal to the newly converted Indians. More than that. There were the many extraordinary things which had happened on his journeys. Rumor even had it that once, when a boat had been lacking to carry him across the great Paraguay River, he had taken off his worn traveling cloak, stepped upon it as though it were a raft, and then proceeded calmly to the opposite shore!

Another wonder had taken place one time when a swarm of wild locusts hovered like a black cloud over the Indians' crops, threatening to devour them. Francis had ordered the locusts to leave, commanding them not even to alight. Immediately they all left!

"If only people would realize that it's God's power, not mine, which works these wonders!" Francis often sighed. "And for the one reason that souls may be won to the Faith! But they don't seem to see below the surface. . ."

Yes, Francis knew that both Indians and Spaniards regarded him as a saint and wonder-worker, and the knowledge weighed heavily upon him. So did the fact that he was Custos of Tucumán. If only he might go about his missionary duties as a simple friar, unburdened by the cares of a superior! If only there were no need for him to give orders to others, to travel from one mission outpost to the next making sure that previous orders had been obeyed!

"Dear Lord, please let someone else be Custos!" he often prayed. "Truly, I believe that I could do much better work for You in some minor position..."

It was not until 1601, however, when he had been a missionary for eleven years, that the heart-felt prayer finally was granted. Then a message arrived from the Commissary General in Lima, Father Anthony Ortiz, stating that Francis was no longer Custos of Tucumán. Another friar had been appointed to the position. As for Francis? Why, he was to come to Lima at once. He had been appointed Vicar of the Friary of Saint Mary of the Angels!

Poor Francis! He was happy enough about being relieved of the responsible post of Custos. Yet his new post as Vicar was a responsible one, too—second only to that of the Father Guardian.

"When I explain things to the Father Commissary, perhaps he'll give me some lesser duty," Francis thought hopefully. "Oh, surely he must understand that I can do much better work for souls when someone tells *me* what to do, instead of the other way around!"

Since his early days in the Order Francis had always dreaded holding a position of authority, believing that he could never discharge the various duties properly. Of course no one could understand such an attitude, for always he had made an excellent superior—first as Novice Master in Arizafa, then as Guardian in Montoro, and finally as Custos of Tucumán. Now what was more natural, since he was being recalled to Lima, than that he should serve in some other important position?

But Francis could not see things this way. Only two facts were of comfort to him as he said good-bye to his beloved Indians and to the other friends he had made during his eleven years as a mission-ary. First, that he was leaving the mission field solely because of his vow of obedience (and hence in submission to God's Will); second, that his work in Lima was to be at the newly built Friary of Saint Mary of the Angels.

"I've heard that this is the home of real saints," he told himself happily. "Oh, dear Lord, thank You so much for the chance to live here!"

It was true that very holy souls resided at Saint Mary of the Angels, for it was a house of recollec-tion. That is to say, to it came those friars who wished to follow the Franciscan Rule in its strict form. And so that this might be more readily accomplished, generally no one left the grounds or engaged in preaching, teaching or other active works. Instead, the friars spent themselves in prayer and penance. And why? So that when the time came for them to go out into the world, either as missionaries or in some other priestly capacity, their souls would be enriched with new grace. They would be more Christ-like, and thus better able to understand and to help their neighbor.

On the 1,400-mile journey from Tucumán to Lima (by way of Chuquisaca and Potosí) Francis often considered the type of life which soon would be his. Actually he had hoped to spend the rest of his days among his beloved Indians. But of course mission work was difficult, and he was not as strong as formerly. No doubt the Commissary General had realized this, and had decided that a fifty-one-year-old friar would be better off at home than wandering through the wilds of Argentina and Paraguay.

"Yet I can still be a missionary in spirit," he thought, "especially since I'm going to live at Saint Mary of the Angels. After all, it's largely because of the prayers and sacrifices of those living there that the active work of the Order is blessed. Dear Lord, with Your grace I hope to give myself completely to this new life! Then perhaps You'll bless the work of some other missionary as You've blessed mine all these years. . ."

It was around June of 1602 when Francis finally completed his arduous journey and arrived in Lima. He was warmly greeted by his brethren, all of whom were anxious to hear of his missionary labors. But it was some time before he could bring himself to speak about these with any zest. On the long trip from Tucumán to Lima he had grown somewhat accustomed to the idea of serving as Vicar. But now, how dreadful! He had just discovered that the Father Guardian was old and sickly, and that the full burden of that office would fall upon his shoulders. Actually, *he* was to be the Father Guardian, and the important work of directing the house of recollection was to be his!

"I'd like to speak with the Father Commissary," he ventured more than once as the friars clustered about him, eager to hear of his missionary experiences. "I'd like to speak with him *privately,* too, if at all possible. . ."

But the Commissary General, Father Anthony Ortiz, guessed the real reason behind the request and saw to it that there was no immediate interview. Tucumán—what was it like? Were the Indians of the district proving loyal to their new Faith? And what about His Lordship, Ferdinand de Trejo y Sanabria, Bishop of Tucumán? Was he well? Had he sent any messages to his old friends in Lima? Surely so, for having been Provincial as well as Guardian at the Friary of San Francisco, he would know how eagerly news of him was awaited.

Francis answered the many questions as best he could. But as the minutes passed, he realized only too well that there was little chance of being relieved of his responsible post at Saint Mary of the Angels. In some way an exaggerated account of his success in missionary work must have reached Lima, for it was very evident that the Father Commissary believed him capable of accomplishing any priestly duty quickly and well.

Naturally this was cause for distress on Francis' part. Yet he adjusted himself to his new duties more easily than he had expected. What a truly peaceful spot was Saint Mary of the Angels! Outsiders, realizing that it was a place of even more prayer and penance than the average friary, probably shuddered on passing by its high-walled inclosure. How dreadful to think that a few steps away lived men who had taken upon themselves a career of suffering and hardship, who interrupted their sleep every night to rise and pray together for two hours, who fasted the greater part of the year, whose silence was almost perpetual!

"Ah, but they don't understand," Francis thought, reveling in the new opportunity to remain before the Blessed Sacrament for long periods of prayer. *"Suffering is hard only when we try to escape from it, not when we go out freely to meet it."* To Francis this was the whole secret of the religious life—or of any Christian life. Suffering, freely embraced for love of souls (as Christ had embraced it), was painful, of course, but quite free of sorrow in the ugly sense of the word. And why? Because once a person has died to his own will, there is nothing more to lose and everything to gain. And how wonderful to know that by a free offering of oneself in suffering, one can win many souls for Heaven!

"How nice if everyone in Lima could understand this, even the little ones!" Francis told himself. "Then the city would be such a happy place..."

But, he reflected, it was most unlikely that the average person in Lima would ever be won to comradeship with suffering. Through ignorance most would go through life afraid of it—fearing sickness, accident, loss of fortune—never glimpsing the great peace which the Heavenly Father has in store for those who give themselves completely to His Will and who freely accept the trials and troubles which He sees fit to send or permit.

"Perhaps sometime I'll give a little sermon on this," he decided. "I think it might do some good."

But right now there would be no sermons, Francis realized, at least to the general public. He had retired from active life in the world. What time he had left from prayer must be given over to his duties as Vicar. And as the months passed there was even less free time, for Francis was removed from the post of Vicar and appointed Father Guardian of Saint Mary of the Angels.

The newly arrived Commissary General, Father John de Monte Major, could not understand why the appointment should be such a cross. "Actually you've been holding this position for months," he said kindly. "As Vicar, and with the Father Guardian in poor health..."

"But it wasn't really the same, Father! I did the work, of course, but everyone knew that I was only substituting for Father Guardian. Now, though..."

"Now, though, *you're* the Father Guardian. And I'm sure that you'll continue to do splendidly in this 'new' post."

Francis hesitated, then clasped his hands pleadingly. "You...you don't suppose I might be relieved of it, Father? I mean, before I begin? After all, there are many others better suited to the work..."

The Commissary General stared in amazement. Then he shook his head. "I'm afraid that things will have to stay as they are," he said. "At least, for the time being."

It was only a few months later, however, that he realized his mistake. The responsibilities of office were proving too much for Francis. His health had been weakened more than anyone had realized by eleven years on the missions. Unless he could lay aside the burden of Guardianship, and very soon, he would collapse.

"I think you need a change, Father Guardian," the Commissary General announced one day. "How would you like to go away for a while?"

Francis hardly knew what to say. He was deeply disappointed in himself for not being able to carry out the duties of his office. And he was very tired. Yet to go away...to leave Saint Mary of the Angels...

Suddenly he fell upon his knees. "Do with me whatever you wish, Father," he murmured. "I know I've been a dreadful failure here."

Quickly the Commissary General raised Francis to his feet. "You've never been a failure," he said reassuringly. "The only reason I want you to go away is to have a good rest. And do you know where I believe your health would improve?"

Francis sighed wearily. "No, Father."

"In Trujillo. The climate up there is good, and with no cares you'd soon be yourself again."

At these words an expression of joyful amazement crossed Francis' face. *Trujillo!* He might go to the beautiful city near the ruins of Chan Chan which Father Balthazar had shown to his little group of missionaries over thirteen years ago? He might go there to live—*and as a simple friar?*

His eyes shone with tears of happiness. "It's too much," he murmured, falling once more to his knees before his superior. "Oh, Father! How can I ever thank you for your kindness?"

CHAPTER 14

A YEAR IN TRUJILLO

ONE REASON that Francis was so happy at the prospect of going to Trujillo was that the city was some three hundred miles to the north of Lima—hence, another three hundred miles distant from Tucumán. It was not likely that his name or his successful missionary labors would be well known here, since travelers from the south generally remained in the capital; if they did venture north, it was usually by water, not by land.

Francis' hopes were justified, and for a while he lived quietly and simply with his brethren in Trujillo. After a few weeks he was in better health than he had been in many years. Then came a distressing message from the Friary of San Francisco in Lima. Another Commissary General had just arrived from Spain—Father John Venido. He was much pleased by Francis' record as a missionary and as superior, but he was not at all pleased by his desire to remain hidden.

"God gives us our talents to be used," he wrote. "Father Francis, it is my wish that in Trujillo you use your talents to the best possible advantage. I want you to take over the duties of Guardian at once—and without objections of any sort."

Poor Francis! At first it seemed that he could not bear the burden which suddenly had been placed upon him. Surely the Father Commissary must know, even if he were a newcomer, that until just recently he had been in poor health and had been sent to Trujillo for a rest? And, more important, that he was better fitted for a humble position than an important one? Then realizing only too well that such thoughts were temptations against obedience, he banished them from his mind.

"I'll do my best to be a good Father Guardian here," he told himself slowly. "But oh, dear Lord! You *must* help me. . ."

So it was that very soon Francis became one of the best-known figures in Trujillo. Regularly he heard Confessions, preached in church and public square, and went about begging for provisions for the community. As a result, he gained a fine understanding of conditions in the city. In the temporal sphere all was well, for the majority of the Spanish colonists had prospered in the New World and Trujillo boasted many fine homes and public buildings. There were beautiful churches, too, as well as monasteries, orphanages and hospitals—all erected by public alms. Yet, strangely enough, the spiritual life of Trujillo was by no means thriving. The people were careless, and generally the churches had but small congregations for Mass or other services.

"It shouldn't be like this," Francis thought.

ONLY A FEW PEOPLE WERE IN CHURCH.

"Through ignorance people are wasting their time. Oh, if they only knew the value of one Mass, how they would crowd the churches!"

On November 12, eve of the Feast of Saint Didacus, Francis was thinking even more seriously about Trujillo's lukewarmness in spiritual matters. Finally he decided that the next morning he would preach in the public church attached to the friary. He would do his best to show those present that time is given to us by God for one reason only: so that we may learn to know, love and serve Him in this world and thus merit the privilege of being happy with Him forever in Heaven.

After his own Mass the next morning, Francis mounted into the pulpit. As he had expected, only a few people were in church. But this did not discourage him. If he could make just one of these souls understand the value of time—that it is a coin wherewith one purchases either Heaven or Hell—his efforts would not have been wasted. And how wonderful if he could also make that same person understand a little about the Holy Sacrifice of the Mass: that it is the one perfect prayer which man can offer to God. . .that through its merits anyone's sins, no matter how many or how dreadful, are atoned for in full measure. . .that it is capable of winning the most wonderful graces for man, woman or child. . .

With a prayer to the Holy Spirit for enlightenment, Francis began to address the handful of people before him. Eagerly, lovingly, he urged that they make their lives more fruitful. They must get others to come with them to Mass in the morning. There must be prayers in common in each home. They must think often of how death would put an end to the time for meriting God's grace. And who could know when death would strike?

So fervently did Francis speak that a few of his listeners, eager that friends and neighbors in shops just outside the church should also hear his words, slipped quietly from their place and went in search of them. Thus, as the minutes passed, word of what was taking place at the Franciscan church spread like wildfire throughout Trujillo. Father Francis Solano was preaching a sermon! And what a sermon! Heaven, Hell, sin, judgment...he was describing each with extraordinary clarity, urging his listeners to amend their lives while there was yet time.

"If we don't change our ways, the good friar says that Trujillo's going to be destroyed by an earthquake!" whispered a pale-faced merchant to a friend who came hurrying into the church halfway through the sermon. "He says there'll be nothing left, not even of this church, unless it might be the pulpit where he's standing!"

The friend glanced quickly about the rapidly filling church, then suppressed a smile. "Don't let Father Francis frighten you," he said. "He's been teaching the Indians for years. This is just one of his little tricks to gain attention."

But this was not mere oratory. Suddenly, miraculously, Francis had been given a glimpse into the future. In about fifteen years Trujillo was to be destroyed by an earthquake. Nothing would remain of the fine homes and beautiful public buildings save a mass of crumbled stone and twisted beams. And why would such a tragedy occur? Because the people of Trujillo were a stiff-necked, obstinate lot. They had no real love of God. If they did pray from time to time, it was only for worldly blessings. There was no concern about the more important things Heaven was waiting to give them.

"Oh, my friends, why can't we beg God to let us know Him better?" Francis cried, stretching out his arms eagerly. "Why can't we ask for more faith? More love of neighbor? More sorrow for sin? These are graces He always grants. And the more fervently we ask for them, the more fully they are poured out upon us. Then, how easy to save our souls..."

The people of Trujillo listened in amazement to the passionate outburst. Indeed, before the day was over a good many had gone to Confession. However, the vast majority, although moved by Francis' words, found excuses to remain away. After all, who was to say if the Father Guardian was right and that the city was to be destroyed by an earthquake? Then again, why should God be so angry with the men and women of Trujillo as to wish to destroy their city?

"People here are no worse than in Lima, Cuzco or Arequipa," objected a well-to-do-merchant. "Believe me, I've traveled to these places and I know what I'm talking about. Father Francis should have brought that out."

"Yes," agreed a companion vigorously. "And I

don't like the way he kept talking about penance.
'We ought to fast every so often on bread and water
because of our sins,' he said. Why, that sort of thing
can ruin a man's health!"

"That's right," put in a third voice. "And did you
hear what he said about children? He'd even have
them doing penance, too. As though their little sins
amounted to anything!"

Suddenly a fourth voice spoke up. "If anyone's
to do penance, why can't it be friars and nuns?
After all, when these men and women went into
the religious life it was to pray and suffer for the
rest of us, wasn't it?"

So the talk went—some upholding Father
Francis' assertion that Trujillo was in a bad state
and that God's anger could be turned away only by
prayer and sacrifice—others insisting that he
painted too black a picture of conditions in the city.
But on his knees in the privacy of his own cell
Francis knew that he had not exaggerated. Trujillo
was doomed. And frequently the saying of the great
Carmelite, Mother Teresa of Jesus, flashed across
his mind in all its startling simplicity:

*"One perfect soul can do more for God's glory
than a thousand ordinary souls."*

Ah, how true these words were! And yet how piti-
fully few understood or cared about them!

"Heavenly Father, please let me make *some* people understand and care," he prayed, "especially
men and women living in the world. Yes, and children, too. Let me show them that they can become
perfect souls by giving themselves completely to

You. And let me show them that you are so pleased when they ask for this wonderful grace of abandonment that You never fail to hear their prayers. . ."

Thus it was that regularly and fervently Francis spoke to the citizens of Trujillo on the matter of perfection—in the church, the marketplace, whenever he found a little group gathered together. *Perfection!* In one sense it had a frightening sound, he admitted. It implied a state so far removed from the average person as to be impossible of attainment. Yet this was not so. The Heavenly Father was perfect. And those who would give themselves to Him without reserve would have taken a long stride towards sharing in that perfection. Then—how beautiful life would become! And death! Never again would there be reason to find fear in either one. . .

As the weeks passed, many in Trujillo were carried away by Francis' words and made a real effort to give themselves into the hands of the Heavenly Father to do with as He willed. They repeated the offering each day and asked for the grace to be faithful to it. Naturally Francis was very happy to be such an instrument of God's grace.

How good it was to be a priest of God! To bring souls to Him! But Francis' work in the city of Trujillo was not to last very long. Toward the middle of 1604, when he least expected it, word arrived that the Provincial Chapter in Lima had appointed him to his former position as Father Guardian of Saint Mary of the Angels. He was to return at once. Another friar would come to Trujillo to assume the duties of Father Guardian.

As best he could, Francis stifled his dismay at the thought of the responsibilities awaiting him and began to prepare for the three-hundred-mile journey to Lima. However, although he did keep his feelings hidden, the friars of Trujillo knew the truth. Father Francis Solano would have preferred the lowest place in the community to the one he had held until just recently with them—or the one to which he was going. For some mysterious reason his soul suffered torments whenever he was placed in a position of authority.

Like the other friars, young Father Paschal realized all this and determined to do what he could to help his beloved superior. Until just recently he had lived at the larger friary of the Order in Lima, known as San Francisco. And not only had he lived there. He had enjoyed the experience. To him, the capital of Peru was a fascinating place, and he had never tired of going about the streets doing what he could for the poor and needy. Oh, how wonderful if obedience would send him back there some day as it was now sending Father Francis...

"Lima's a city of great saints," he declared earnestly as he came upon the latter making ready for his trip. "You spent a year there, Father Guardian. Don't you agree?"

Francis looked up in surprise. Had he heard correctly? Lima was a city of great saints?

"When I visited with the Archbishop after my return from Tucumán I was much impressed by his sanctity," he admitted slowly. "I don't think I've ever seen a holier face. And of course I've heard of the wonders he's done for those in need. But I would hardly say that there was more than one such heroic soul in Lima, Father." Then, after a moment's pause: "Or is there?"

With difficulty the younger religious controlled the joy that suddenly surged within him. His suspicions had been right! For some strange reason Father Francis did not know about Lima's other holy citizens. But in a little while he would. God willing, in a little while he would be so eager to go to Lima to meet them that he would have forgotten most of his fears concerning the Guardianship of Saint Mary of the Angels.

"It's generally understood that there are two other saints in Lima besides Archbishop Turibius, Father Guardian. Haven't you heard of Brother Martin de Porres who lives with the Friars Preachers at Santo Domingo? Or of young Rose de Flores who lives at home with her family?"

Francis shook his head. "I'm afraid not, Father. You see, I spent only one year in Lima, and that year at Saint Mary of the Angels. As you know, it's a place of retirement and prayer. Gossip from the outside world..."

Father Paschal nodded understandingly. "Yes, but it's hardly on account of gossip that everyone in Lima loves Martin and Rose, Father Guardian. Why, the Viceroy himself is Martin's close friend. And the city treasurer, Don Gonzalo de Massa, is like a second father to Rose. And why?"

Francis smiled. "Why, Father?"

"Because these two young people are so closely united to God that He grants anything they ask of Him. For instance, I myself know that Brother Martin has cured at least three hopeless invalids by his prayers; that he can read the secrets of hearts as though they had been spoken aloud. As for Rose de Flores. . ."

Suddenly a light flickered in Francis' eyes. "You say that these saintly souls are young people?" he asked slowly.

"Yes, Father Guardian. If I'm not mistaken, Martin was twenty-four last December 9. And Rose was eighteen a few weeks ago—on April 30. Oh, I could tell you so many wonderful things about each one!"

For a moment all was silence. Then Francis indicated that his companion should be seated. "Why not do so?" he asked. "Begin at the beginning, Father. And who knows? Perhaps I'll forget my own cares in listening to what you have to tell me about God's young friends."

For just a moment something in these words caused Father Paschal to hesitate. Could it be that there was a twinkle in the Father Guardian's eye? That the little scheme to bring him comfort and consolation on the eve of his departure for Lima had been understood from the beginning?

Quickly he thrust the suspicion from him. "It's this way," he began calmly. "Martin is the son of a white Spaniard, Don Juan de Porres, and a freed black slave from Panama, Anna Velasquez. At the age of fifteen he went to Santo Domingo to be a servant to the friars there. Then just the other day,

CHAPTER 15

THE GREAT SERMON

S O EAGERLY did Father Paschal tell of the black lay Brother's remarkable spiritual gifts that Francis was carried out of himself. What a wonderful person the young man must be! And Rose de Flores as well, whose special joy it was to care for sick Indian women within her own home and whose exquisite flowers were eagerly sought after in Lima's public market.

"Perhaps some day there'll be a chance to meet Martin and Rose," he told himself. "How wonderful that would be!"

But once returned to Lima, Francis soon found that he had no time for visiting—even with God's chosen ones. In addition to the hours of prayer and meditation each day at Saint Mary of the Angels, the Father Guardian must also spend himself in many other ways—in supervising various works, in conferences with this friar or that—encouraging, consoling, advising. As a result, he had almost no free time for himself.

"If I did have some free time, I'd like to go out

and preach," he thought. "But right now perhaps
it's just as well that I stay here at home. To preach
well, a man must have something to say—
something he has learned in prayer. And somehow
I feel that these days God wants me to be on my
knees listening to what He has to tell me, rather
than going out talking to others."

So the weeks passed—the cold, damp weeks of
July and August—the warm, springlike weeks of
September, October, November. Francis remained
at Saint Mary of the Angels, fulfilling his numerous
duties as well as possible and striving always to follow the promptings of the Holy Spirit which
resulted from his meditations. Then one day shortly
before Christmas he knew that the time to preach
had come. The many hours of prayer finally had
produced fruit and God wished that this fruit
should be passed on to others.

Around seven o'clock that same evening, after a
few minutes of fervent recollection before the
Blessed Sacrament, Francis went in search of the
lay Brother who had charge of the gate.

"Brother Porter, I'm going out," he said gently.
"Will you recommend me to the Lord so that
tonight I may render Him an important service?"

The Porter stared. *Father Guardian was leaving
the friary? And at night?* Why, this was almost
unheard of! Yet being well-grounded in obedience,
he quickly recovered himself. "May the Lord bless
you this night, Father," he said earnestly. "May He
bless your work, too."

Quietly, then, Francis set out. His destination

was Lima's public market, a mile or so distant from the peaceful cloisters of Saint Mary of the Angels. If all were as usual, he told himself, there would be a good crowd there tonight. The market would be full of business activity after the oppressive heat of the December day. Spaniards, Negroes, Indians —all manner of men would crowd into the torchlit dusk—buying, selling, eating, drinking. There would be music and dancing, too, with the spirit of the world in plain evidence.

"But no one will be thinking of You, Heavenly Father," he murmured. "No one will be thanking You for the gift of life, for Baptism and the other Sacraments. Why, before the night is over there'll even be souls defying You and Your Commandments! Unless. . .oh, Heavenly Father, unless *You* give me the right words to touch their hearts!"

As he walked, Francis' fingers sought out the wooden missionary cross which he had thrust into the cord about his waist before leaving home. Lovingly he regarded the crudely hewn piece of wood.

"Please let me be of some use to You tonight," he whispered. "Through the merits of Your Son's death on Calvary. . ."

By the time Francis had reached the market, the theme of his sermon was clear. God was love, yet man was constantly thwarting that love. Many times this was because of thoughtlessness, but there were also countless times when it was because of sheer selfishness, and even malice. Well, atonement for sin must be made by means of penance.

"Unless you do penance, you shall all likewise

perish," Our Lord had said to His disciples.

"I will say these words, too," Francis thought. "Oh, Heavenly Father, may they help some souls tonight to turn away from sin!"

Naturally many at the market were astonished when they saw the Father Guardian of Saint Mary of the Angels making his way through their midst. Since his return from Trujillo he had appeared in the streets only rarely, and certainly never in the evening. Then in a little while there was even more astonishment. Father Francis had not come to buy for his friars, or even to beg. He had come to preach!

At first, however, since business was brisk, not much heed was paid to his words. Merchants vied with one another in calling out the merits of their wares while customers argued noisily for a lower price. Beggars whined for alms. Babies cried. Dogs barked. Donkeys brayed. Older children ran in and out of the crowd intent upon their games. Music was everywhere—weird tunes played by Indian musicians on their wooden flutes, gay Spanish rhythms played on guitar and tambourine. At the various food stands succulent rounds of meat sizzled and sputtered as they turned over slow fires. Then suddenly a thunderous voice rang out above the noisy and carefree scene:

"For all that is in the world is the concupiscence of the flesh, and the concupiscence of the eyes, and the pride of life, which is not of the Father but is of the world."

It was as though a bombshell had fallen. At once

the hubbub died away, and hundreds of Lima's startled citizens turned to where a grey-clad friar, cross in hand, had mounted an elevation in the center of the marketplace and now stood gazing down upon them with eyes like burning coals. But before anyone could wonder about the text from Saint John's first epistle, Francis began to explain the meaning of concupiscence: that, because of Original Sin, it is the tendency within each person to do evil instead of good; that this hidden warfare will end only when we have drawn our last breath.

"If we were to die tonight, would good or evil be the victor within our hearts?" he cried. "Oh, my friends! Think about this question! *Think hard!*"

Within just a few minutes Lima's marketplace was as hushed and solemn as a cathedral. All eyes were riveted upon the Father Guardian and all ears were filled with his words as he described God's destruction of the ancient cities of Sodom and Gomorrha because of the sins committed within them.

"Who is to say that here in Lima we do not deserve a like fate?" he demanded in ringing tones. "Look into your hearts now, my children. Are they clean? Are they pure? Are they filled with love of God?"

As the minutes passed and twilight deepened into darkness, the giant torches of the marketplace cast their flickering radiance over a moving scene. As usual, crowds of people were on hand, but now no one was interested in buying or selling. Instead, faces were bewildered, agonized, fearful. Tears

LIMA'S MARKETPLACE WAS AS HUSHED AND
SOLEMN AS A CATHEDRAL.

were streaming from many eyes as Francis' words continued to pour out in torrents, urging repentance while there was still time.

"Can we say that we shall ever see tomorrow?" he cried, fervently brandishing his missionary cross. "Can we say that this night is not the last we shall have in which to return to God's friendship?"

As these and still more terrifying thoughts struck home one after another, the speaker stretched out both arms, bowed his head, and in heartrending tones began the Fiftieth Psalm. At once the crowd was filled with fresh sorrow and made the contrite phrases their own:

"Have mercy on me, O God, according to Thy great mercy.

"And according to the multitude of Thy tender mercies, blot out my iniquity.

"Wash me yet more from my iniquity, and cleanse me from my sin.

"For I know my iniquity, and my sin is always before me.

"To Thee only have I sinned, and have done evil before Thee: that Thou mayest be justified in Thy words, and mayest overcome when Thou art judged . . ."

Soon wave upon wave of sound was filling the torchlit marketplace as priest and people prayed together. Then Francis preached again, doing his best to implant a still greater sorrow for sin and an even firmer purpose of amendment in the hearts of his hearers. Finally, looking neither to right nor to left, he prepared to depart for Saint Mary of the

Angels. But on all sides men and women pressed about him, sobbing and begging for his blessing.

"Father, please pray for me!" cried one young girl. "I've deserved to go to Hell a thousand times!"

"Last year I robbed a poor widow of ten pounds of gold!" declared a swarthy-faced Spaniard. "May God forgive me!"

"I'm worse than anyone," moaned a wild-eyed black man. "Tonight I was going to kill a man...*and for money!*"

So it was that first one, then another, cried out his fault and expressed a desire to go to Confession at once. But Francis had to refuse all such requests. Yes, he was a priest. It was his privilege and duty to administer the Sacraments. But he was also a religious, and bound by rule to various observances. One of these was that he must be in his cell at Saint Mary of the Angels by a certain hour each night.

"There are other priests in the city who can help you, though," he said kindly. "Go to them now, my children. And may the Holy Virgin bring you back to her Son without delay."

It was with a happy heart that Francis finally took his departure from the marketplace. Surely God had blessed his preaching? From all appearances everyone who had heard him speak was now eager to make amends for sin.

"Thank You, Heavenly Father," he whispered as he made his way back through the darkened streets to Saint Mary of the Angels. "It was very good to be Your tool tonight."

But although Francis felt that he had preached

a successful sermon, he never dreamed to what an extent his listeners had been affected. Nor that Divine Providence had ruled that his references to Sodom and Gomorrha should be misunderstood and everyone convinced that Lima was about to be destroyed, too. No, silent and grateful he returned to his friary in the foothills outside the city, gave the Brother Porter an understanding smile of thanks for his prayers, then retired to his cell.

It was a different matter within Lima itself, however, and before an hour had passed, the Cathedral and the various parish churches were crowded with fearful penitents.

"The city's going to be destroyed by an earthquake!" one awed voice told another. "Father Francis said so!"

"No, fire and brimstone will fall from Heaven," was a second version. "Both the innocent and wicked will die in torment!"

"It's the end of the whole world, not just of Lima!" declared still a third group. "Oh, may God have mercy on us. . ."

By midnight the various rumors had multiplied to such an extent that the city was in a panic. Even the members of the various religious Orders were terror-stricken. If Father Francis Solano had prophesied that Lima was to be destroyed for its sins, it must be so. He was a saint. Look at the wonders he had performed as a missionary—the discovery of a spring of fresh water in the midst of an arid countryside; the cure of hundreds of sick and crippled; the conversion of nine thousand

Indians by one sermon . . .

"Oh, let's confess our sins while there's time!" was the message that went from one monastery to another. "Let's do penance as Father Francis said!"

Very soon the darkened streets of Lima began to glow like chains of jewels as the Blessed Sacrament was carried in torchlight procession from one parish church to the next. Without exception, the men and women taking part in the processions were barefoot, and groaned and beat their breasts as they recited the Seven Penitential Psalms. A few, anxious to do even greater public penance for their faults, carried heavy crosses on their shoulders. Others, garbed in sackcloth, walked with ropes about their necks as though they were common criminals on their way to the gallows. Fearful that at any minute God would send an earthquake or some other calamity to destroy their city, the people of Lima had laid aside their pride and now were giving themselves wholeheartedly to expiation. Even children joined in the penitential processions from one church to another, and there was not a confessional anywhere that was empty.

Still more striking was the eager spirit of amendment. On all sides ill-gotten goods were being restored. Enemies of many years' standing asked no questions but became reconciled to one another on the spot. Scores of marriages were being rectified, children baptized, debts paid, lies acknowledged, for there was no telling when the dreadful earthquake would strike—or the fire and brimstone fall from Heaven.

"Out of the depths I have cried to Thee, O Lord; Lord, hear my voice," came the sobs of the women penitents as they made their way through the streets.

"Let Thine ears be attentive to the voice of my supplication," replied the troubled voices of the men.

"If Thou, O Lord, wilt mark iniquities, Lord, who shall stand it?"

"For with Thee there is merciful forgiveness; and by reason of Thy law I have waited for Thee, O Lord..."

So it went, with fear and sorrow increasing by the minute. Finally the Viceroy (who governed Peru in the name of the King of Spain) grew worried. Surely some weaker souls in the city would be driven insane unless something were done to calm the panic! Accordingly, he arranged for a meeting in his palace with the Archbishop and the Commissary General of the Franciscan Order. Perhaps the three of them together could work out some kind of a solution. A proclamation, for instance, setting forth God's mercy as well as His justice in dealing with sinners...

Strangely enough, the Commissary General knew nothing of the sermon which Francis had preached some hours before, although various people—both lay and religious—had attempted to explain the reason for the penitential processions through the streets, the crowds waiting to go to Confession, the great wave of penitence sweeping the city. But overcome with impatience, he had turned away abruptly. Lima was to be destroyed by an earth-quake? Fire and brimstone would fall from Heaven? The end of the world was at hand? Why, surely this was only childish gossip! Who but God knew the future—of Lima, or of any other city?

Yet now, realizing that it was Father Francis who had been the source of all the commotion, he turned impulsively toward the Viceroy. "Your Excellency, we must bring the good man here," he declared. "And we must ask him to repeat what he can of the sermon he gave in the marketplace. You see, it may be that people misunderstood his words. Or, without realizing it, that he was carried out of himself when he spoke on death and judgment."

The Viceroy nodded gravely. "I wanted your per-mission, Father Commissary, before I took official steps. But since it's so late. . ."

The Commissary General shook his head. "The friars at Saint Mary of the Angels will be saying Matins now, but send your officers there just the same. Tell them to bring Father Francis to us at once. This is a serious matter."

CHAPTER 16

THREE WORDS. . .AND SOME OTHERS

THE FRIARS of Saint Mary of the Angels were amazed and not a little anxious when they saw the Viceroy's soldiers escorting their Father Guardian from the chapel in the midst of Matins. But Francis himself was not alarmed. The Archbishop, the Father Commissary and the Viceroy wished him to come to the latter's palace and repeat what he could of the sermon he had given in the marketplace? Very well; he would do so.

Thus it was that before the most important group of men in Peru—the Royal Council—Francis presently was repeating his sermon. Once again he held aloft his missionary cross. Once again he described the goodness of God, the dreadful pride of man in setting himself up against the divine laws, the great need of penance to atone for such faults. Even more. So vividly did he portray the destruction of Sodom and Gomorrha, those wicked cities of the Old Testament where penance had been absolutely unknown, that fear filled every heart.

The Viceroy and his advisors, even the Commissary General and the saintly Archbishop Turibius, were overcome. How clearly Francis showed the dreadfulness of sin. Even venial sins—oh, they were never to be regarded lightly! And by mortal sin, a mere creature actually scorned the God Who had made him out of the slime of the earth, given him an immortal soul and the chance to be happy in Heaven forever.

"Unless you do penance, you shall all likewise perish!" cried Francis as his illustrious audience shuddered for still another time at the enormity of sin, the inescapable instant of judgment, the eternity of Heaven and Hell. "Indeed, can we say that we shall ever see tomorrow? Can we say that this night is not our last for returning to God's friendship?"

In a few minutes some of the Viceroy's counsellors could control themselves no longer. Leaving their places, they threw themselves at Francis' feet and earnestly entreated him to hear their Confessions.

"Please pray that the earthquake won't come until I can be with my wife!" cried one. "Oh, Father Francis! Ask God to let us die together. . ."

"And my little ones!" implored another. "Their mother is already dead, and they have no one but me! Oh, Father Francis, won't you hear my Confession and let me go to them while there's still time?"

In amazement Francis gazed at the prostrate figures before him—at the pale and anxious faces of the Viceroy, the Commissary General, the Archbishop, the other noble and learned members of the Royal Council. Then with startling suddenness he realized what had happened—here and at the marketplace. God had permitted that his two sermons should have their most unusual effect so that both priests and people would do penance. Twice, within a few hours' time, He had given a poor friar's words superhuman power, so that even now the streets were echoing to the cries of thousands of penitents as they made their way from one church to another. . .praying, weeping, groaning; so that even now one richly furnished chamber in the Viceroy's palace was filled with the terrified leaders of Lima's political and religious groups.

"Listen, my friends," said Francis, in far gentler tones than he had been using. "I think that an explanation is in order."

So it was that very soon the members of the Royal Council were being reassured as to their spiritual and temporal well-being. There was no need to be afraid, Francis said. God did not intend that their beautiful city should be ruined by earthquake. The only question of ruin was that pertaining to souls who persisted in sin. And for these, the ruin would be far more dreadful than any human words could describe. It would consist of the pain and loneliness of Hell—*forever!* But as for those present, and those making their way from one church to another in the penitential processions outside? Ah, all was well! God was pleased with their humility and contrition. Even now He was flooding their souls with many choice graces.

"Then surely we should tell them this, Father!"
cried the Viceroy in a joyful burst of relief. "Surely
a proclamation, quoting what you have just said. . ."

Francis nodded. "By all means issue a proclamation, Your Excellency. Post it in all the public
places. But in the meantime, have no fear. God has
been really glorified these last few hours."

True enough. During the night, as closely as anyone could estimate, some eight thousand citizens
of Lima had been to Confession and had taken
upon themselves extraordinary works of penance to
atone for their own sins and for the sins of others.
Three thousand marriages had been rectified, and
countless children baptized. As for the value of the
stolen goods restored, the number of enemies
reconciled, calumnies revoked, debts paid, painful
admissions made—who could begin to reckon
these?

"There was never anything like it to happen in
Lima since the city was founded, almost seventy
years ago," declared the Viceroy as he hastened
to make out the proclamation. "Surely this night
will go down in history—and Father Francis' name
with it!"

All Lima agreed with the Viceroy, especially
when the reassuring words of the proclamation
greeted their eyes and they realized that God was
not going to visit death and destruction upon them
in a matter of minutes or even of hours.

"But we must use our time well," one person told
another, pondering the last line of the proclamation
wherein the Viceroy counselled the people to give

up their sinful lives so that never again could Lima be compared to the wicked cities of Sodom and Gomorrha. "And what's the best way to use time?"

There was considerable argument on this point. In the fervor of their recent conversion, many now believed that the only proper way to use time was in lengthy prayer upon one's knees. Again, that God could be served in a fitting way only by priests and religious consecrated to His service.

"But what about married people?" cried one young woman. "Can't parents with little ones to care for please God, even though they haven't time for long prayers?"

"What about those of us who have to work to support ourselves and others?" put in a middle-aged man. "We haven't time for long prayers, either."

"Yes, and what about old people?" ventured another voice. "And the sick? And children?"

In the end a little group determined to go to Saint Mary of the Angels and ask Father Francis what to do. They had been much impressed by his sermon in the marketplace, and they were really anxious to lead good lives and not fall into sin again. But because they were neither priests nor religious, with a superior to obey and a rule of life to follow, it was hard to know where to begin.

"Surely Father Francis can help us," they said.

The Father Guardian was pleased with his visitors. Having offered a brief prayer to the Holy Spirit for enlightenment, he proceeded to give them his views on the best way of using time. No, it was not necessary for a man or woman to be a priest or religious in order to use time well and be pleasing to God. Nor was it necessary to spend long hours in prayer each day. But, if one wanted to go to Heaven more easily and more surely, it was necessary to spend *some* time, five minutes or so each day, in a conversation with the Heavenly Father, and in this same little conversation to offer oneself to Him in union with His Son.

"Many days the Devil will make it very hard to spend even that short while talking with God," he admitted. "He'll send distractions; he'll make your minds and bodies feel tired even before you begin; he'll disturb you in a hundred irritating ways. But there'll be no success for the Devil if, in these times of trouble, you'll remember to address three special words to the Heavenly Father. Now—have you any idea as to what these words are?"

The little group made several attempts to discover the three words, but without success. Then, smiling happily, Francis came to the rescue.

"They're very simple," he said. "When prayer seems difficult or useless, just turn to the Heavenly Father and say: 'Here we are!' "

The men and women gathered about Francis stared in reverent awe. What tenderness in his voice! What happiness in his eyes! Yet what did he mean? How could these three simple words, "Here we are," overcome the Devil? Unless, of course, they possessed miraculous powers. . .

Before any questions could be asked, however, Francis was explaining the truly wonderful value of the three words that soon were to form the basis of his friends' daily conversations with God. Of course there was no reason why each person present could not say "Here *I* am, Lord" to the Heavenly Father and so offer himself to the Divine Will—even as the boy Samuel had done in the Old Testament. It was a splendidly humble action, and one which God certainly would bless. But was it not much better to be living in the days of the New Testament? Was it not much better (by virtue of Bethlehem and Baptism) to be able to come before the Heavenly Father with Christ as the All-Perfect Companion and Brother? Was it not much better to be able to change Samuel's words and say them thus: "Here *we* are"?

"That's our privilege since the first Christmas night," Francis declared happily, "when the Son of God took upon Himself our human nature and became man. Oh, my friends, just think! When we are in the state of grace, Jesus Christ is in our souls. He is with us every minute of the day and night, helping us to become holy with His holiness. Truly, we make a wonderful gift to the Heavenly Father when we offer ourselves, and Christ within us, to do His Will!"

Once again the little group was lost in reverent awe. So this was the meaning of "Here we are"! Then finally one young man spoke up. "Is. . .is this the way to use time well, Father Guardian? You mean that each day for a little while we should have a. . .a *conversation* with the Heavenly Father?"

Francis nodded. "Yes. If you spend five minutes

in this way, your whole day will be sanctified. You see, Christ will add His infinite merits to yours when you say to His Father 'Here *we* are.' Then the Heavenly Father will not see just *you*—human, weak, imperfect. He will also see His Son in you. And He will pour forth His love upon both of you."

"But the Devil! Didn't you say that the three words have some kind of power to drive him away?"

Again Francis nodded. "Yes, that's what I said. The Devil has very little success with souls who use those three words faithfully, offering themselves to the Heavenly Father in union with Our Lord."

In due course the visitors took their departure. And in a very serious frame of mind. For it was a new idea, this suggestion of saying "Here we are" to the Heavenly Father for a brief period every day. On the surface it seemed almost too simple a practice to be worthwhile. . .

"But I'm going to try it," declared one man resolutely. "After all, Father Francis is a saint. Certainly any advice of his must be really good."

"Yes," observed his wife, "I have an idea that if we say those three words every day as he suggested, God will grant us many wonderful blessings."

"I agree with you," put in a second woman. "And how comforting to think that if we give ourselves in prayer to the Heavenly Father for just five minutes, if we say 'Here we are' as fervently as we can, why then our whole day is made worthwhile. Really, I don't think that I ever heard anyone say that before!"

"I know I never did," said the first speaker slowly.

"And what a pity! If I had known about 'Here we are,' I might have used thousands of hours to really good advantage."

Before long many others were saying the same thing, and Francis' skill as a spiritual director became even more widely known throughout the city. Dozens of men and women sought him out for advice and encouragement, and without exception all were introduced to the custom of offering themselves to the Heavenly Father in union with His Son for a short period of time each day. "Here we are" became truly famous words.

Then one morning while he was walking among the palm trees in the friary garden, Francis saw still another penitent coming toward him. This was a grey-haired man, richly dressed but obviously in poor health, who leaned heavily upon a cane.

"Bless me, Father, for I have sinned!" said the newcomer, a bit awkwardly. "May I. . .may I go to Confession?"

For just a moment Francis stared in amazement. This wan-faced stranger! Surely it couldn't be his old friend John? John, who had been his fellow novice in Montilla? John, who had left the religious life some thirty-six years ago and come to the New World for fame and fortune?

"But it *is* you, old friend!" he exclaimed, expressions of joy and anxiety crossing his face. "And you're not well! Oh, John! What's happened? Why haven't you come to see me before this?"

In half an hour most of the story was out. After years of struggle (during which he had drifted away from the practice of his religion many times), John was now one of the wealthiest men in Peru—and back in the Church. His gold and silver mines yielded a small fortune every month. He had been to Spain twice in the last seven years, attending to various investments there. His oldest son was married, and in charge of the family's mining interests in Cajamarca. The second son was also married and established in Potosí, where a fine new vein of silver had just been discovered. But the third son, eighteen-year-old Thomas. . .

"Yes?" said Francis encouragingly. "What about him, John? He was just a little fellow when I saw him on my one visit to your house. Remember?"

John nodded. Francis' visit had occurred fifteen years ago, in 1590, when he was on his way with Father Balthazar and three other friars to the mission fields of Tucumán. The group had been spending a short while in Lima then, recovering from the effects of the shipwreck in the Gulf of Gorgona. . .

"Yes, I remember, Francis. And although I do want to go to Confession, it's really because of Thomas that I've come. You see, unless something's done, that boy is going to break my heart. . .and his mother's."

"What?"

"That's right. He heard your sermon in the marketplace the other evening. Now he says we mustn't expect him to be like his brothers, interested in worldly success. All he wants is to enter one of your friaries and study to be a priest."

At these words a soft radiance came into Francis'

eyes. "But that's wonderful, John!"

The latter shook his head grimly. "No, it's not wonderful. Why, until he heard your sermon the other night, Thomas was just the usual rich man's son—interested in amusements, reckless companions, adventure. Now he's just the opposite. Daily Mass, visits to the Blessed Sacrament, prayers of all sorts. All very unnatural. But of course it'll never last."

"No?"

"No. And why should it? It's not right for the boy to be thinking of the religious life. He's needed at home, especially with his brothers gone away and his mother and I growing old. . ."

Francis said no more. But as he set himself to listen to the rest of John's story, his eyes were increasingly thoughtful. Truly, pride was the greatest weed in the garden of the soul. In John's case it had been growing steadily for years, forcing him to acquire ever greater wealth and power. Right now, of course, with his goal reached and his health broken by constant strain and planning, he scarcely seemed the arrogant creature who once had refused an alms to a little beggar boy in the Plaza. Yet was he really changed? In the depths of his soul (despite the fact that he had returned to the practice of his faith) was he not still very proud and selfish? Although he had never admitted it to anyone, had not his own failure as a religious always rankled? Was he now not fearful that his youngest son would also fail to persevere, and so bring back painful memories?

As he prayed for the necessary light and strength

to help his friend, Francis felt the urge to enlarge upon the great grace of a religious vocation. Well he knew that many parents do not understand this when it comes to their own sons and daughters. Finally, however, Francis set aside the important topic in favor of another.

"John," he said suddenly, "have you and your wife ever considered becoming Franciscans?"

The latter gasped with astonishment. What was this? He, to be a friar once again? His wife, to enter the Poor Clares?

"Of course not!" he cried indignantly, while a wave of color swept his pale face. "Francis, what an idea!"

Francis smiled. "You misunderstand me, old friend. I was not thinking of religious life in the strict sense. I was thinking of our Third Order for lay people. You know, membership there might solve many of your problems."

"*Problems?* But I've only one problem—Thomas and his foolish idea that he wants to be a friar! And so far you haven't told me what to do."

Francis smiled again. "I know. But suppose you let me tell you about our Third Order for lay people. After that, it may be much easier to talk about your boy."

"HAVE YOU AND YOUR WIFE EVER CONSIDERED
BECOMING FRANCISCANS?"

CHAPTER 17

THE PASSING YEARS

AT FIRST JOHN had little interest in hearing about the Franciscan Third Order for lay people, commonly known as the Order of Penance. Yet as Francis explained its purpose—that men and women living in the world might share in all the good works of the Franciscan friars and nuns (provided they were faithful to a simple rule of life)—he found himself strangely moved. Could it be that despite his many lapses from grace he was called to be a son of Saint Francis after all? That in the midst of great wealth he should suddenly glimpse the blessing of being poor in spirit?

"I don't understand what's happening to me," he confessed suddenly. "Francis, what is it? What spell are you working?"

Francis smiled, recalling that faraway day in the novitiate in Montilla when he had first decided to pray that somehow, some time, his friend might return to the Franciscan family and become a priest. He had been faithful to that prayer for many years—until the meeting with John in the Plaza and the discovery that he was married. But it had been only a short time later when he had resumed his prayer again...and this time with the Third Order for lay people in mind. Yes, God willing, John would still be a Franciscan—*a Franciscan Tertiary*—one of the many thousands of men and women in the New World who had affiliated themselves with the Order of Friars Minor so that they might lead a more Christian life.

What if John had drifted away from the practice of religion? All was not lost. God's grace was so wonderful! In an instant a lifetime of evil could be forgiven in the Sacrament of Penance. And of course many a contrite sinner was numbered in the ranks of the Franciscan Tertiaries...even among those called Blessed by the Church.

But Francis did not put such thoughts into words now. Instead, he took his friend's hand. "I have no spell," he said, "but God has many. Suppose you come to Confession and see which one He has destined for you today?"

Before an hour had passed, John was a changed man. Suddenly, almost miraculously, the scales were falling from his eyes and he was seeing the world and everything in it in a new light. One truth was especially evident: *that only by being rooted in God, by having faith in Him instead of in creatures and things, can a person be truly happy.* The saints had known this, of course, and had been governed accordingly. His friend Francis, too. But he? Oh, how stupid he had been!

"It's not too late for me to change, though," he

told himself as he made his way homeward. "With God's grace, even a great criminal can save his soul in a few seconds by being truly sorry for his sins. Oh, Heavenly Father! Thank You for letting me understand this! Thank You for giving me a friend like Francis! And if it's Your Will that my boy should be a priest and a religious. . .thank You for that, too—*oh, so much!*"

Naturally John's wife was amazed at the truly unexpected conversion. To think that her husband should be interested in becoming a Franciscan Tertiary, and that he wanted her to become one, too! That he now insisted he was going to build a fine chapel in honor of the Blessed Virgin if Thomas should be ordained a priest!

"It's nothing short of a miracle," she confided to her friends. "Surely Father Francis is a saint to have done all this?"

"Of course he's a saint," declared one woman. "Why, he's always working wonders of one sort or another—especially when it's a question of saving a soul. Or of helping someone in trouble."

"That's right," put in another. "In that respect he's just like our wonderful Archbishop. God lets His power shine forth in each of these good men so that sinners will come to Him through them. Oh, may they both be with us for a long, long time!"

Alas for this heartfelt prayer! On March 23, 1606, while on the third visitation of his huge Archdiocese, Turibius Alphonsus de Mogrovejo, second Archbishop of Lima, breathed his last in the distant village of Saña. He was sixty-eight years old, and had labored for souls in his adopted America since the year 1581.

"But Lima still has three saints," men and women told one another hopefully. "Father Francis Solano, Brother Martin de Porres, Rose de Flores. . ."

Yes, despite their sorrow over the Archbishop's passing, everyone was consoled by the thought that the friary of Saint Mary of the Angels possessed an heroic soul in Francis; likewise the Monastery of Santo Domingo in its Negro lay Brother, Martin; and the family of Gaspar de Flores in its beautiful young daughter, Rose.

"Yet how long will matters stay this way?" various shrewd observers asked one another. Rose de Flores and Brother Martin were still young—twenty and twenty-seven years old, respectively. But Father Francis had just celebrated his fifty-seventh birthday on March 10. And surely in recent days his health had not been all that it should be?

"The responsibility of being Guardian is wearing that good soul down," one friend told another. "Oh, if only the Commissary General would realize this and let him be a simple friar once again!"

The heartfelt wish was unexpectedly granted. Although Francis had not been talking about his failing health, within a few weeks after the death of Archbishop Turibius he was informed that his duties as superior were over. Even more. He would no longer follow the strict rule of life which was in force at Saint Mary of the Angels. Instead, he would go to live in the larger friary of the Order in Lima, commonly known as that of San Francisco.

The news that now he was just a simple friar, with no pressing responsibilities of office, was cause for great joy on Francis' part. In one way or another, much as his human nature had rebelled against the idea, he had spent the greater part of his religious life in charge of souls. As Novice Master in Arizafa and later in the friary of San Francisco del Monte; as Guardian in Montoro; as Custos of Tucumán; as Guardian at Saint Mary of the Angels and later of the friary in Trujillo; then back again to Saint Mary of the Angels. . .

"Now all that's over and done with?" he asked eagerly of the Commissary General.

"Now it's all over and done with," was the heartening reply. "We want you to have a rest, Father Francis. A real rest."

So for the first few weeks in his new home, Francis rested. That is, he took no extra labors upon himself but merely followed the simpler community exercises. But then he grew uneasy. Was it right to be taking such care of his body when all about him souls were in need of spiritual help and encouragement?

"I'd like to go out and preach a little tomorrow," he said to the Father Guardian one afternoon after Vespers. "May I, please?"

The latter hesitated. These days Father Francis was looking much better, but certainly his strength had not returned completely. The effects of eleven years of missionary work could not be set aside that easily. Besides, there had also been the great mental strain during the periods when he had served as Guardian of Saint Mary of the Angels and in Trujillo. Now, bearing all this in mind...

"It would be just little talks that I'd give, Father Guardian," said Francis reassuringly, reading his superior's uneasy thoughts. "Here and there on the street corners...perhaps a little music for the children..."

In the end, the Father Guardian was won over to Francis' point of view. Street preaching, if it were undertaken for brief periods at a time, probably would do him no harm. Nor playing little tunes on his violin for Lima's young folks. But he must have a companion on these excursions from the cloister. Brother John Gomez must go along to see that he did not tire himself, either in preaching or in playing.

"God be praised!" cried Francis, his eyes shining with new happiness as he realized that he had just been given permission to work for souls once more. "I must go and tell Brother John to be all ready for tomorrow! Thank you, Father Guardian! Thank you so much!"

The Father Guardian smiled. "God be praised!" —the familiar motto of the Franciscan Order—had always had an amazingly joyful ring whenever spoken by Father Francis. But surely the way he had spoken it just now could make even the saddest person glad to be alive?

"God be praised!" he replied quickly. "Be sure to take good care of yourself, my son."

The days that followed were happy ones for

Francis—and instructive ones for his companion, Brother John Gomez. Almost every morning the two set out for a short walk through the city. Brother John carried Francis' violin, and occasionally he was able to get his beloved friend to tell something of how the now dilapidated instrument had helped to make conversions during the many years of labor in the jungles of Tucumán.

One day he was particularly successful in this venture. "You'd go out at night, wouldn't you, Father, when the Indians were dancing and feasting about their bonfires, and start to play?"

At these words Francis' eyes twinkled. How Brother John loved mission stories! Especially the more thrilling ones where God's goodness had allowed a poor friar to convert entire tribes with just one sermon...to pass unscathed through deep forests where wild animals and poisonous reptiles abounded...to walk over raging torrents as though on dry land...to cure hopeless invalids...even, oh, wonder of wonders, to raise the dead to life!

"Yes," he said, looking fondly into Brother John's eager eyes, "I often went out at night, Brother, to do what I could for souls. And if there was an eclipse of the moon, I never missed. You see, always at these times the poor Indians thought that the moon was dying, and were beside themselves with fear. And when they heard the violin playing in the darkness, they were even more fearful. The Great Spirit was abroad! He had come to make them slaves!"

"But you soon showed them otherwise, didn't

you, Father? You came out from among the trees and explained about the eclipse, and that there was no need to be afraid. And then you began to tell the Indians about God...and in a little while all of them were your friends...and they told other Indians about you...and word went through the jungle that there was only one God...*your* God...and thousands of men and women and children came to be baptized...and you sent other friars to look after them as soon as you could..."

Francis was far from being carried away by this flood of enthusiastic words. Instead, he laid an affectionate hand upon his companion's shoulder. What a good soul this was! So innocent! So child-like! "It was something like you say, Brother," he admitted slowly. "But of course we must never forget one thing."

"Yes, Father? What is it, Father?"

"That success as a missionary, or in any other line of activity which has God's glory for its aim, is largely due to the prayers and sacrifices of others. Why, *you* had, and have, a really important part in converting the Indians of Tucumán!"

Brother John's eyes widened with surprise at such an unexpected statement. "*I*, Father? But how can that be? I've never been to Tucumán! In fact, I don't even know where it is!"

"Perhaps not. But you often say little prayers for the missionary friars, don't you? An Our Father? A Hail Mary?"

"Well..."

"And sometimes you make little sacrifices? You

don't let anyone know how tired you are after a hard day's work in the garden? You keep back impatient words when there is good reason to say them? You give away fruit to another Brother, even though you very much want to enjoy it yourself?"

Slowly Brother John's face flooded with color. "Those. . .those are just little things, Father. Any child can do them."

"Of course. But don't overlook their value. Because you offer those little prayers and sacrifices to the Heavenly Father in union with the merits of His Son's sufferings and death upon Calvary, they are tremendously valuable. Oh, Brother John! I *know* that little acts like these won for me the grace to do good work for souls when I was a missionary! And I know, too, that they're doing the same for other priests right now."

Brother John was not the only one whom Francis encouraged to pray and make sacrifices for the missions. The children of Lima, his special friends, were likewise inspired in the little talks he gave to them on the street corners, on the steps of public buildings, wherever he could find a few youngsters gathered together.

"Play for us so we can dance, Father!" these cried whenever they saw him coming.

"Yes, and sing for us, too, Father. *Please!*"

Always Francis agreed to his young friends' requests. But there was one condition. First, each boy and girl must listen carefully to a little lesson from the Catechism. Afterward would come the music and the dancing. Even more. Whoever could

ALWAYS FRANCIS AGREED TO HIS
YOUNG FRIENDS' REQUESTS.

give the best explanation of the day's lesson would
be allowed to take Father Francis' violin in his
hands and have a brief instruction in how to play
upon it.

"There's no one to understand souls like this
good priest," Brother John Gomez told himself, as
day after day new crowds of children gathered
eagerly about the grey-clad friar. "Oh, if only these
young people knew how fortunate they are to have
him for a teacher—and a friend!"

Despite his frequent preaching in Lima's streets,
Francis' health grew no worse. Indeed, since he
never complained of feeling tired or sick, it finally
was taken for granted that he had recovered from
the hardships of life in the mission fields. Thus one
year passed, two years, four years, during which he
continued to reside at the Friary of San Francisco
—preaching, hearing Confessions and otherwise
spending himself for the welfare of souls. By now
his sermons were given in all manner of strange
places—outside of shops, in theatres, at bullfights
—wherever men and women gathered together for
business or for pleasure. And as usual the sermons
produced extraordinarily good results.

"And why shouldn't they?" Brother John asked
his friends more than once. "Before Father Francis
ever sets foot outside the friary on these preaching
trips, he kneels down before the crucifix in
church."

"Yes? And what does he say there, Brother?
Some special prayer?"

"Prayer? Well, not exactly. He looks and thinks."

"Looks and thinks?"

"Yes. About Calvary. And in a little while the most wonderful thoughts come to him...about how much God loves us...about His kindness to sinners...the joys of Heaven...oh, all sorts of ideas occur to Father Francis which he puts into his sermons to help ordinary people become holier and happier. You see, he's always said that the crucifix is the most wonderful book in the world, with all the truths that a wise man needs to know. Not a day passes that he doesn't go to look at it with real love and devotion."

So earnestly did Brother John speak of Father Francis' many virtues that it was easy to see that he was one of his most fervent admirers. Then one May morning in the year 1610, when Francis was sixty-one years old, the devoted lay Brother experienced a sudden and sickening shock. There would be no preaching trip through Lima's streets today. His beloved friend was too ill to rise from his bed...

"He's dying," he thought incredulously, as he went in rapid search of the Father Infirmarian. *"Dying!"*

CHAPTER 18

THE SONG

NATURALLY THERE was great consternation in the friary at the news that suddenly and unexpectedly Father Francis had collapsed, and that his pulse was weak. Priests and lay Brothers, novices and Tertiary helpers were beside themselves at the thought that death might come for their good friend at any moment. But the Father Guardian, believing that somehow he had failed in his duty toward Father Francis, took the news harder than anyone.

"I don't understand it!" he kept saying over and over again. "Father Francis seemed to be in good health . . . he never complained of pain . . . he never asked to be excused from any duties . . ."

Peter Rodriguez and Martin Sanchez, Lima's outstanding doctors, nodded sympathetically. "It's not your fault, Father Guardian. Undoubtedly the good man was ailing for weeks, but he never complained because he wanted to keep on working for souls."

"But . . . but this is dreadful! He shouldn't have been out preaching every day . . . walking miles and miles...hearing Confessions at all hours..."

"No, Father Guardian."

"If I had understood how things really were, I'd have made him rest..."

"Of course you would. But you mustn't worry about that now, or you'll be sick yourself. Just remember this: we're going to do everything that we can to help Father Francis. *Everything!*"

"How...how long do you give him to live?"

"About a week. His heart is too worn out to last any longer."

Another opinion came from the Infirmary, however. In a voice that was scarcely above a whisper, yet filled with joy for all that, Francis declared that the doctors were quite mistaken. He would live much longer than a week. In fact, God would not call him for two months—until July 14, the Feast of Saint Bonaventure.

"The Heavenly Father is so good!" he told Brother John Gomez with a smile. "He's letting me be a missionary for a little while longer."

"A *missionary*, Father?" whispered the latter brokenly.

"Yes. I won't be preaching during these next two months, but I'll be suffering. And I've always found that that's the best way to win souls for Heaven."

Poor Brother John! How his heart ached at these words, for suddenly he felt himself miles apart from his beloved friend. Suffering might be the best way to win souls for Heaven, but surely only a saint could see it in its true light and embrace it willingly...even with longing! Surely the average person could look upon suffering only with dread, for himself or for his loved ones. . .

"No, Brother John," said Francis, seeming to read his thoughts. "God will grant a love of suffering to all who ask for it. The trouble is that hardly anyone—men, women or children—ever thinks of praying for such a grace. And what a pity it is!"

"A pity, Father?"

"Yes. Because when a person loves suffering and knows how to offer it to the Heavenly Father for souls, fear goes out of that person's life. He is born again, as it were. Oh, my brother! If I could make just a few people understand this before I die—that when they take suffering to their hearts as a price-less gift from God—when they give up their wills and accept it freely as Christ did, for love of souls—then real joy is theirs to keep. . .*always!*"

Brother John hardly knew what to say. Francis' face, tired and drawn with pain as it was, actually was glowing. And his eyes. . .ah, how they shone! Then words did come—slowly, awkwardly.

"I've. . .I've always been a coward, Father. Surely you don't mean that such a person as I could learn to love suffering?"

Francis stretched out an understanding hand. "Why not? All that's necessary is to ask the Heavenly Father for this wonderful grace."

"But. . .but I'm not sure that I really want it!"

Despite his weakness, Francis smiled. "It's the Devil who's making you talk like this," he said. "He doesn't want one of God's choicest gifts to come your way. But don't pay any attention to him,

Brother. Ask the Heavenly Father, in the Name of His Son, to give you a love of suffering so that you can do great things for souls. Ask for this priceless grace every day. Then see how much happier and more peaceful your life will become."

Even as he was considering the suggestion, Brother John suddenly realized that it was time for him to report for work in the kitchen. And that their talking together had all but exhausted his beloved friend's strength.

"Father, I've got to go now," he said contritely. "And I'm very sorry if I've tired you. But how I do thank you—*for everything!*"

Very slowly Francis lifted his hand in blessing. "It's all right, Brother. Come back when you can. Then we'll have another little talk about suffering. You know, it's one of the least understood things in the world—and one of the most important!"

For the rest of the day Brother John could not get these words out of his mind. What a splendid man was Father Francis! And no wonder he had been so successful as a missionary. He was a true hero, unafraid of any suffering, believing that it could win souls for Heaven. How astonishing was his insistence that there was nothing extraordinary about this lack of fear, that God was eager to give it to anyone who asked for it—man, woman, or child!

"It must be so," Brother John told himself firmly. "Oh, suppose I do what he suggested! Suppose I ask the Heavenly Father for a love of suffering, so that I can be of use to others too!"

Before a week had passed, Brother John was a changed man. Never had he thought to experience such peace and joy as that which now flooded his soul. The trials and troubles coming his way these days were not the disagreeable things they once had been. They caused pain, yes. They were against nature. Yet suddenly he was seeing them in their true light—opportunities sent by the Heavenly Father whereby he might merit graces for himself and for others with each passing minute.

"What a mistake people make when they don't ask God to give them a love of suffering!" he told himself. "Since life is so full of it anyway, it's much better to accept it willingly and without fear—something even a child can do, with His grace. Oh, to think of all the times that I relied upon my own strength when suffering came. . .and then ran away from it. . .and of how little good the running away did me in the end!"

Brother John was not the only one to learn a valuable lesson at Francis' sickbed. As the days passed, scores of others profited from visits there, including the Viceroy and his attendants, the members of the Royal Council—even Bartholomew Lobo Guerrero, successor to Turibius as Archbishop of Lima. Indeed, it soon became evident that the New World's most famous missionary was bent on using his last remaining strength in God's service. At the age of forty, and at the height of his powers, he had come to America to preach the True Faith to the Indians of Tucumán. Now, twenty-one years later, sick and dying, to his fellow-countrymen in Peru. . .

"Just to look at Father Francis is worth any number of sermons," declared the Viceroy humbly. "What love of God is in his eyes! What joy! Oh, when I think of all the mornings he permitted me to serve his Mass. . ."

"Certainly there's no one like him," admitted the Viceroy's son. "Why, whenever he gives me his blessing, I can really feel God's grace pouring down upon me."

As the chilly days of June gave place to the equally chilly days of July, it seemed that no one in Lima could talk of anything save Father Francis Solano, his accomplishments and approaching death. What wonderful things he had done for souls since coming to America! And how rightly was he called "The Apostle of Tucumán" because of his eleven years of work among the Indians in this section of northern Argentina.

"When he had his headquarters at the friary in Talavera, he must have made hundreds of trips into the jungle in quest of souls," one person told another in awed tones. "Even into the Gran Chaco."

"That's right. And there's no more dangerous country in the whole continent than that of the Gran Chaco."

"I know. Some people call it 'the Green Hell.' But Father Francis was never a man to be stopped by danger. He went there several times."

"Yes, as far as the Paraná and Paraguay Rivers, and even beyond. But I think he deserves another title besides that of 'The Apostle of Tucumán.' "

"What?"

"Why, 'The Apostle of Peru.' After all, look what he's done for souls here."

It was true. During the last eight years, Francis had accomplished an enormous amount of good in Trujillo and Lima by his preaching and spiritual direction. Now that he was dying, there was sorrow in both cities, but particularly in Lima.

"To think that never again will I hear the good man playing on his violin!" sobbed an old woman whom Francis had been accustomed to visit from time to time. "It. . .it just doesn't seem possible!"

Her little grandson did not understand such a statement. Or the tears. "Father Francis will tell some more of his wonderful stories the next time he comes, Grandmother. Truly he will. Then you'll feel much better."

The old woman caught the boy to her heart. "Bless you!" she murmured. "You're too young to understand what a sad day is in store for all of us."

But at the Friary of San Francisco, made as comfortable as possible by Brother John Gomez (the Father Infirmarian's new assistant), Francis had no fears about his approaching death. Indeed, he awaited the Feast of Saint Bonaventure with childlike eagerness.

"Heaven!" he whispered over and over again. "To see God face to face! To know Him as He really is! To be with the Saints and Angels! To be perfect ourselves! Oh, Brother John. . .are there any words in the whole world to describe how wonderful it must be?"

The latter, wincing at the very thought of being separated from his beloved friend, shook his head. "No, Father," he whispered. "There. . .there aren't any words."

Francis could not help catching the sorrow in Brother John's voice—as well as the light in his eyes which showed that he was doing his best to bear it for love of souls—and for a moment he gazed tenderly upon him. In many ways, he reflected, Brother John was like another friend of his, dead these many years. Yes, Brother John was as gallant a figure as Father Bonaventure, the young priest who, during the plague in Montoro, had turned his cowardice into strength by giving himself completely to the Will of the Heavenly Father.

But then his thoughts faded away, and he closed his eyes wearily. Brother John leaned forward anxiously. "Father! You're all right? You're. . .you're not. . ."

There was a dreadful interval of silence. Then slowly Francis stretched out a reassuring hand. "No, I'm not dying yet, Brother. But I want you to listen carefully. I've a message for you. . .a message that I want you to give to as many souls as you can. . .when I've gone from you."

Brother John choked back a great sob. "What. . . what is it, Father?"

"Just this. I've always loved music. Even as a boy, some of my happiest hours were spent in singing and playing the violin. Many times I made up the melodies myself, simple little things. . .some gay, some sad. . ."

"Yes, Father. I've often heard your songs."

"But now I know that just one song is worth-while, Brother. Just one song on earth can even begin to compare with the beautiful songs of Heaven."

There was silence in the little room as Brother John gazed at Francis in astonishment. Surely this couldn't be the message he was to give to others! Why, what did it mean? *One song?* Yet even as he tried to understand, Francis nodded slowly.

"Yes, Brother, that's right. One song. And anyone can learn to sing it, just as you have done."

"*I*, Father?"

"Yes. Oh, surely you understand what I mean?"

And then suddenly all was quite clear. The song was the song of joy—the song that comes naturally to every soul which has given itself to the Heavenly Father to do with as He wills and so no longer fears suffering. Since early boyhood Francis had under-stood about this song. Its heartening melody had been with him through years of trial and hardship. Now, having taught it to Brother John, he wanted him to tell others about it, to help them realize its wonderful power to make every life, no matter how drab, into a thing of holy beauty.

"You will tell people about the song, Brother? You see, I can't do it myself anymore. . ."

Brother John brushed away a tear. "Of course I'll tell them, Father! But please say you'll be with us for a long time yet! Oh, much longer than the Feast of Saint Bonaventure!"

Francis shook his head. "No, Brother. That will

be my last day on earth."

Early in the morning of July 14 it was evident that Francis' strength was all but gone. Two days before, he had received the Last Sacraments. Since then, small groups of anxious men and women had formed the habit of gathering about the friary from time to time in order to obtain word of their beloved friend's condition. Now, however, the little groups had suddenly turned into an immense and sorrowing throng that lined the street for blocks and could not be dispersed.

"Please pray for me when you go to Heaven, Father!" sobbed a woman's voice.

"Yes, and give me good health, Father!" cried her husband.

"My boy! Keep my boy from harm and send him back to me!" implored an old woman tearfully. "Please, Father Francis!"

"Help me to save my soul!" begged still another voice.

Within the friary itself, however, there was a more tranquil atmosphere. Priests and Brothers came and went in noiseless procession from the infirmary. Nor did anyone seem surprised that just outside the infirmary window dozens of small brown birds should be fluttering about, twittering and chirping as though it were a springtime feast day and not a chill winter morning when Lima was about to lose one of her greatest citizens.

"My little friends!" whispered Francis, smiling faintly at the birds. "Oh, if we could just praise God as faithfully as these tiny creatures do. . ."

"MY LITTLE FRIENDS!" WHISPERED FRANCIS,
SMILING FAINTLY AT THE BIRDS.

As the hours passed, a group of priests and Brothers gathered about Francis' bed to recite a variety of Psalms and hymns. The voices rose and fell in peaceful rhythm, and several times it seemed that the dying man had drifted into sleep. But towards eleven o'clock, he roused himself.

"Father Guardian," he murmured. "I'd like. . ."

At once the Father Guardian arose from his knees. "Yes, my son? What would you like?"

"To hear the Creed once more. . ."

Immediately everyone present began to recite the Apostles' Creed, that ancient prayer which contains the chief articles of faith, and which Francis had taught to so many thousands of Indians.

"I believe in God, the Father Almighty, Creator of heaven and earth. . ."

But as these words were reached: *"Who was conceived by the Holy Ghost, born of the Virgin Mary,"* Francis suddenly flung wide both arms in the form of a cross. His face was radiant, glowing, not at all like that of a dying man.

"God be praised!" he cried triumphantly.

Quickly Brother John Gomez arose from his knees. A saint had just finished his song. Now it was time to teach the wonderful melody to others.

St. Meinrad, Indiana
Tuesday in Holy Week
April 16, 1946

By the same author . . .

6 GREAT CATHOLIC
BOOKS FOR CHILDREN

. . . and for all young people ages 10 to 100!!

1137 THE CHILDREN OF FATIMA—And Our Lady's Message to the World. 162 pp. PB. 15 Illus. Impr. The wonderful story of Our Lady's appearances to little Jacinta, Francisco and Lucia at Fatima in 1917.   8.00

1138 THE CURÉ OF ARS—The Story of St. John Vianney, Patron Saint of Parish Priests. 211 pp. PB. 38 Illus. Impr. The many adventures that met young St. John Vianney when he set out to become a priest.   12.00

1139 THE LITTLE FLOWER—The Story of St. Therese of the Child Jesus. 167 pp. PB. 24 Illus. Impr. Tells what happened when little Therese decided to become a saint.   8.00

1140 PATRON SAINT OF FIRST COMMUNICANTS—The Story of Blessed Imelda Lambertini. 85 pp. PB. 14 Illus. Impr. Tells of the wonderful miracle God worked to answer little Imelda's prayer.   6.00

1141 THE MIRACULOUS MEDAL—The Story of Our Lady's Appearances to St. Catherine Labouré. 107 pp. PB. 21 Illus. Impr. The beautiful story of what happened when young Sister Catherine saw Our Lady.   7.00

1142 ST. LOUIS DE MONTFORT—The Story of Our Lady's Slave. 211 pp. PB. 20 Illus. Impr. The remarkable story of the priest who went around helping people become "slaves" of Jesus through Mary.   12.00

1136 ALL 6 BOOKS ABOVE (Reg. 53.00)   THE SET: 43.00

U.S. & CAN. POST./HDLG.: $1-$10, add $2; $10.01-$20, add $3; $20.01-$30, add $4; $30.01-$50, add $5; $50.01-$75, add $6; $75.01-up, add $7.

At your Bookdealer or direct from the Publisher.
Call Toll Free 1-800-437-5876

More books by the same author . . .

8 <u>MORE</u> GREAT CATHOLIC BOOKS FOR CHILDREN

. . . and for all young people ages 10 to 100!!

1230 SAINT PAUL THE APOSTLE—The Story of the Apostle to the Gentiles. 231 pp. PB. 23 Illus. Impr. The many adventures that met St. Paul in the early Catholic Church.   13.00

1231 SAINT BENEDICT—The Story of the Father of the Western Monks. 158 pp. PB. 19 Illus. Impr. The life and great miracles of the man who planted monastic life in Europe.   8.00

1232 SAINT MARGARET MARY—And the Promises of the Sacred Heart of Jesus. 224 pp. PB. 21 Illus. Impr. The wonderful story of remarkable gifts from Heaven. Includes St. Claude de la Colombière.   11.00

1233 SAINT DOMINIC—Preacher of the Rosary and Founder of the Dominican Order. 156 pp. PB. 19 Illus. Impr. The miracles, trials and travels of one of the Church's most famous saints.   8.00

Continued on next page . . .

At your Bookdealer or direct from the Publisher.
Call Toll Free 1-800-437-5876

1234 KING DAVID AND HIS SONGS—A Story of the Psalms. 138 pp. PB. 23 Illus. Impr. The story of the shepherd boy who became a warrior, a hero, a fugitive, a king, and more.   8.00

1235 SAINT FRANCIS SOLANO—Wonder-Worker of the New World and Apostle of Argentina and Peru. 205 pp. PB. 19 Illus. Impr. The story of St. Francis' remarkable deeds in Spain and South America.   11.00

1236 SAINT JOHN MASIAS—Marvelous Dominican Gatekeeper of Lima, Peru. 156 pp. PB. 14 Illus. Impr. The humble brother who fought the devil and freed a million souls from Purgatory.   8.00

1237 BLESSED MARIE OF NEW FRANCE—The Story of the First Missionary Sisters in Canada. 152 pp. PB. 18 Illus. Impr. The story of a wife, mother and nun—and her many adventures in pioneer Canada.   9.00

1238 ALL 8 BOOKS ABOVE (Reg. 76.00)   THE SET: 60.00

Get the Complete Set!! . . .

SET OF ALL 20 TITLES

by Mary Fabyan Windeatt

(Individually priced—179.00   Reg. set prices—143.00)

1256 THE SET OF ALL 20 . . . . Only 125.00

U.S. & CAN. POST./HDLG.: $1-$10, add $2; $10.01-$20, add $3; $20.01-$30, add $4; $30.01-$50, add $5; $50.01-$75, add $6; $75.01-up, add $7.

At your Bookdealer or direct from the Publisher.
Call Toll Free 1-800-437-5876

TAN BOOKS AND PUBLISHERS, INC.
P.O. Box 424
Rockford, Illinois 61105

MARY FABYAN WINDEATT

Mary Fabyan Windeatt could well be called the "storyteller of the saints," for such indeed she was. And she had a singular talent for bringing out doctrinal truths in her stories, so that without even realizing it, young readers would see the Catholic catechism come to life in the lives of the saints.

Mary Fabyan Windeatt wrote at least 21 books for children, plus the text of about 28 Catholic story coloring books. At one time there were over 175,000 copies of her books on the saints in circulation. She contributed a regular "Children's Page" to the monthly Dominican magazine, *The Torch*.

Miss Windeatt began her career of writing for the Catholic press around age 24. After graduating from San Diego State College in 1934, she had gone to New York looking for work in advertising. Not finding any, she sent a story to a Catholic magazine. It was accepted—and she continued to write. Eventually Miss Windeatt wrote for 33 magazines, contributing verse, articles, book reviews and short stories.

Having been born in 1910 in Regina, Saskatchewan, Canada, Mary Fabyan Windeatt received the Licentiate of Music degree from Mount Saint Vincent College in Halifax, Nova Scotia at age 17. With her family she moved to San Diego in that same year, 1927. In 1940 Miss Windeatt received an A.M. degree from Columbia University. Later, she lived with her mother near St. Meinrad's Abbey, St. Meinrad, Indiana. Mary Fabyan Windeatt died on November 20, 1979.

(Much of the above information is from Catholic Authors: Contemporary Biographical Sketches 1930-1947, *ed. by Matthew Hoehn, O.S.B., B.L.S., St. Mary's Abbey, Newark, N.J., 1957.)*